WELFARE: YOUR RIGHTS AND THE LAW

by
Margaret C. Jasper

Oceana's Legal Almanac Series:
Law for the Layperson

2002
Oceana Publications, Inc.
Dobbs Ferry, New York

Information contained in this work has been obtained by Oceana Publications from sources believed to be reliable. However, neither the Publisher nor its authors guarantee the accuracy or completeness of any information published herein, and neither Oceana nor its authors shall be responsible for any errors, omissions or damages arising from the use of this information. This work is published with the understanding that Oceana and its authors are supplying information, but are not attempting to render legal or other professional services. If such services are required, the assistance of an appropriate professional should be sought.

Library of Congress Control Number: 2002113668

ISBN: 0-379-11369-4

Oceana's Legal Almanac Series: Law for the Layperson
ISSN 1075-7376

Manufactured in the United States of America on acid-free paper.

To My Husband Chris

Your love and support
are my motivation and inspiration

-and-

In memory of my son, Jimmy

Table of Contents

CHAPTER 4:
SUPPLEMENTAL SECURITY INCOME

CHAPTER 5:
THE FOOD STAMP PROGRAM

CHAPTER 6:
MEDICAID

CHAPTER 7:
PROMOTING CHILD WELFARE

CHAPTER 8:
THE DEPARTMENT OF HEALTH AND HUMAN SERVICES

APPENDICES

ABOUT THE AUTHOR

MARGARET C. JASPER is an attorney engaged in the general practice of law in South Salem, New York, concentrating in the areas of personal injury and entertainment law. Ms. Jasper holds a Juris Doctor degree from Pace University School of Law, White Plains, New York, is a member of the New York and Connecticut bars, and is certified to practice before the United States District Courts for the Southern and Eastern Districts of New York, the United States Court of Appeals for the Second Circuit, and the United States Supreme Court.

Ms. Jasper has been appointed to the panel of arbitrators of the American Arbitration Association and the law guardian panel for the Family Court of the State of New York, is a member of the Association of Trial Lawyers of America, and is a New York State licensed real estate broker and member of the Westchester County Board of Realtors, operating as Jasper Real Estate, in South Salem, New York. Margaret Jasper maintains a website at http://members.aol.com/JasperLaw.

Ms. Jasper is the author and general editor of the following legal almanacs: Juvenile Justice and Children's Law; Marriage and Divorce; Estate Planning; The Law of Contracts; The Law of Dispute Resolution; Law for the Small Business Owner; The Law of Personal Injury; Real Estate Law for the Homeowner and Broker; Everyday Legal Forms; Dictionary of Selected Legal Terms; The Law of Medical Malpractice; The Law of Product Liability; The Law of No-Fault Insurance; The Law of Immigration; The Law of Libel and Slander; The Law of Buying and Selling; Elder Law; The Right to Die; AIDS Law; The Law of Obscenity and Pornography; The Law of Child Custody; The Law of Debt Collection; Consumer Rights Law; Bankruptcy Law for the Individual Debtor; Victim's Rights Law; Animal Rights Law; Workers' Compensation Law; Employee Rights in the Workplace; Probate Law; Environmental Law; Labor Law; The Americans with Disabilities Act; The Law of Capital Punishment; Education Law; The Law of Violence Against Women; Landlord-Tenant

Law; Insurance Law; Religion and the Law; Commercial Law; Motor Vehicle Law; Social Security Law; The Law of Drunk Driving; The Law of Speech and the First Amendment; Employment Discrimination Under Title VII; Hospital Liability Law; Home Mortgage Law Primer; Copyright Law; Patent Law; Trademark Law; Special Education Law; The Law of Attachment and Garnishment; Banks and their Customers; Credit Cards and the Law; Identity Theft and How To Protect Yourself; Welfare: Your Rights and the Law; Individual Bankruptcy and Restructuring; Harassment in the Workplace; and Health Care and Your Rights.

INTRODUCTION

Prior to the Great Depression, welfare in the United States was virtually non-existent. The catastrophic economic upheaval and massive unemployment that followed necessitated government intervention. The federal government responded by enacting the Social Security Act of 1935 to address these problems.

The Unemployment Compensation program was established to assist the unemployed, and the Social Security program was established to supplement the retirement income of the elderly. Both of these programs are "insurance" program. Deductions are made from an employee's wages to help fund the programs, and when an individual reaches retirement age or becomes unemployed, he or she is entitled to receive monetary benefits as a result of these contributions.

However, the Act also recognized that there were many individuals living in poverty who were not eligible for these programs, and provided for federal grants to support state welfare programs for low-income elderly and families with children. Since that time, many federal and state government public assistance programs have evolved to assist those in need. This almanac explores the historical development of these social welfare programs in the United States.

Major offshoots of the early social welfare programs include Supplemental Security Income (SSI)—a federally administered program which provides monetary assistance to low-income elderly, blind and disabled individuals, and Aid to Families With Dependent Children (AFDC), commonly referred to simply as "welfare." Both of these programs have recently undergone significant revamping. The eligibility guidelines of the SSI program have become more stringent, and the AFDC program was completely overhauled with the 1996 passage of the Personal Responsibility and Work Opportunity Reconciliation Act (the "Welfare Reform Act").

Concern for the health and nutrition of low income families spawned the Medicaid program, which addresses the health care needs of the poor, and the Food Stamp program, which is designed to assist low income families by subsidizing the cost of groceries for those families who meet certain maximum income thresholds. In addition, the United States Department of Health and Human Resources administers hundreds of programs aimed at assisting those individuals who are least able to help themselves, and many such programs are focused on services that assist children and the elderly.

This almanac discusses the law governing the administration of these social welfare programs, which is often confusing and complex. Entitlement issues, eligibility guidelines and restrictions, procedural rules, and related information are also examined in this almanac.

The Appendix provides resource directories, applicable statutes, and other pertinent information and data. The Glossary contains definitions of many of the terms used throughout the almanac.

CHAPTER 1:
HISTORICAL DEVELOPMENT OF SOCIAL WELFARE PROGRAMS IN AMERICA

THE ENGLISH "POOR LAWS"

In 1601, England established the first of its series of "Poor Laws" to help its disadvantaged population. The "English Poor Law of 1601" dealt with the government's responsibility to provide for the welfare of its people. Under this statute, taxes were assessed to fund relief programs which were locally controlled, and "almshouses" were founded to shelter the homeless.

Although the law acknowledged the government's responsibility for the needy, it was also considered harsh in that it viewed the poor as undesirables and treated them likewise. In addition, amongst the poor, there were distinctions made as to which individuals were deserving of aid and which individuals were ineligible.

THE EARLY AMERICAN "POOR LAWS"

When the English-colonists arrived in America, they established "Poor Laws" similar to those they were accustomed to in England. The early colonial laws also used taxation as a means to fund the programs, which were again administered locally. The colonies also distinguished between poor persons who were deemed worthy of assistance, and those who were not eligible for relief.

As the colonies expanded, local control over financial aid to the poor became burdensome, and state assistance was sought. Through the 18th and 19th centuries, "poorhouses" were instituted to shelter and provide relief to the indigent population. However, obtaining such relief was purposely made very difficult in order to discourage dependency on the state. For example, personal property could be forfeited, as well as the right to vote and freely move throughout society. In some cases, those receiving assistance were required to display certain markings on their clothing.

Distributing financial assistance outside of the poorhouses was frowned upon because the citizens did not want to encourage dependency on the state by making it easier to obtain help. However, operating the poorhouses became increasingly expensive, and some financial assistance outside of the poorhouse setting began to occur. Nevertheless, society sought to keep government assistance in this area to a bare minimum.

THE CIVIL WAR PERIOD

The Civil War resulted in hundreds of thousands of disabled veterans, widows and orphans. During that time, the dependent American population was proportionally the largest it has ever been in history. In response to this crisis, a pension program, with many similarities to our current social security system, was developed.

The first piece of legislation was passed in 1862, and provided pension benefits to soldiers who were disabled as a result of their military duty. Widows and orphans were eligible for pension benefits that their parent or spouse would have received had they been disabled. Nevertheless, former Confederate soldiers and their families were barred from receiving Civil War pensions.

By 1890, a military service connected disability was no longer required, thus any disabled Civil War veteran was eligible for benefits and, by 1906, Civil War pension benefits were extended to older Americans. Nevertheless, this forerunner of the modern social security system was not extended to the general population until much later.

THE INDUSTRIAL REVOLUTION

The deterioration of the traditional sources of economic security in America was attributed to cultural and demographic changes which began with the Industrial Revolution. The Industrial Revolution transformed a largely agricultural society to a nation of industrial workers. Thus, individuals could no longer depend on their own hard work to put a meal on the table for their family, but were subject to conditions outside of their control, such as the possibility of unemployment.

In addition, the change from an agricultural society to an industrial society forced many Americans to move from farms to urban areas, and largely accounted for the subsequent disappearance of the extended family—i.e., a household which included grandparents and other relatives. The extended family was beneficial in that the family assumed financial responsibility for any members who became disabled or too old to work.

Another significant and related demographic change which developed was the increase in life expectancy due, in large part, to advances in public health care. As a result, there was a rapid growth in the elderly population, and there were no programs in place to address this growing problem.

THE DEPRESSION ERA

In the 1920's, it was not just the wealthy who invested their fortunes in the stock market. There were many smaller investors who gambled their modest incomes in a system that promised them riches. When the stock market crashed on October 24, 1929, the economic security of millions of Americans disappeared overnight and America slipped into an economic depression.

Welfare benefits for the elderly, and individuals and families with no or low income had been almost non-existent prior to the Great Depression of the 1930's. With millions of people unemployed, the federal government saw income security as a national problem. America's economy was in crisis. Banks and businesses were failing, and the majority of the elderly population lived in poverty.

Out of concern for the poverty-stricken elderly population, approximately 30 states passed some form of old age welfare pension program by 1935 to deal with the crisis. However, benefits under these programs were modest, eligibility was restricted based on income, and many of the programs were inadequately implemented.

There was a public outcry for a federal response to this growing problem, and a number of movements developed, each with a proposed pension scheme. President Herbert Hoover responded that the most effective way to combat economic insecurity was through voluntary relief. Hoover had enjoyed success in international relief efforts, before and after World War I, through the efforts of voluntary partnerships of government, business and private donations.

Hoover believed this kind of "volunteerism" would solve the problems of the Depression. Although he authorized some limited federal relief efforts, his main response to the Depression was to advocate these voluntary efforts. Unfortunately, voluntary charity proved impossible because the nation's wealth had been so profoundly diminished in the three years following the stock market crash.

THE CONCEPT OF SOCIAL INSURANCE—THE ROOSEVELT ADMINISTRATION

President Franklin D. Roosevelt introduced an economic security proposal based on social insurance rather than welfare assistance to address the permanent problem of economic security for the elderly. Social insurance programs had been successfully implemented in many European countries since the 19th century.

Social insurance endeavors to solve the problem of threatened economic security by pooling risk assets from a large social group and providing income to those members of the group whose economic security is imperiled, e.g., by unemployment, disability, or cessation of work due to old age.

Under Roosevelt's proposal, a work-related, contributory system would be created in which workers would provide for their own future economic security through taxes paid while employed. The Social Security program that was eventually adopted in late 1935 relied on this concept of "social insurance."

THE SOCIAL SECURITY ACT OF 1935

The Social Security Act was signed by President Roosevelt on August 14, 1935. Originally, the Social Security Act was named the Economic Security Act, but this title was changed during Congressional consideration of the bill. Under the 1935 law, Social Security only paid retirement benefits to the primary worker. A 1939 change in the law added survivors benefits and benefits for the retiree's spouse and children. The Act also provided for Social Security Disability Insurance (SSDI) for workers.

Under SSDI, if a person has to stop working at any time before age 65 due to health reasons, he or she may be eligible for benefits. However, there are eligibility requirements for SSDI. For example, the disabled worker: (i) must meet the Social Security standard for disability; and (ii) must have worked the required number of quarters for a person their age and contributed to the Social Security system, to qualify for this "insurance" program.

In addition to establishing the two major "social insurance" programs to respond to future income loss—Social Security and Unemployment Compensation—the Social Security Act authorized federal grants to support state welfare assistance to other segments of the impoverished population, including the "needy" elderly, the blind, and the disabled. These three programs were known as the "adult categories." The Act also authorized assistance to low income families with children.

In 1963, a Welfare Administration was established to administer the public assistance programs—which became known as "Aid to Families with Dependent Children" (AFDC). The so-called "adult categories" remained under the jurisdiction of the Social Security Administration, which eventually evolved into a federally administered program for the elderly, blind, and disabled, known as Supplemental Security Income (SSI).

The SSI program is discussed more fully in Chapter 4 of this almanac.

The Department of Health, Education, and Welfare—subsequently renamed the Department of Health and Human Services—was established and designated the parent organization for both economic relief agencies until 1994, when a bill was passed which established the Social Security Administration as an independent agency.

Both the SSI and the AFDC programs were supplemented by two important "in kind" benefit programs also funded by the federal government—Medicaid and Food Stamps. Needy individuals not meeting the eligibility criteria for federal assistance could still qualify for purely state or state and local relief, often called general assistance.

THE WELFARE REFORM MOVEMENT

In 1996, Congress passed the Personal Responsibility and Work Opportunity Reconciliation Act (PRWORA) (the "Welfare Reform Act"). The new law eliminated AFDC and replaced it with "Temporary Assistance for Needy Families" (TANF), which placed permanent ceilings on the amount of federal funding for welfare, and gave each state a block grant of money to help run its welfare program. For example, under the 1996 law, federal funds may only be used to provide a total of five years of aid in the lifetime of a family.

The PRWORA and the TANF program are further discussed in Chapter 3 of this almanac.

Another significant change brought about by the welfare reform movement was the complete exclusion of legal aliens from receiving any SSI benefits. The passage of the Contract with America Advancement Act of 1996 narrowed the number of people allowed to receive SSI disability benefits by requiring that drug addiction or alcoholism not be a material factor in their disability.

The law governing entitlement to any one of these welfare programs is complex. For individuals or families involved with more than one of them the situation is even more so. Federal law applies to federal benefits like SSI and in some respects, to federally funded benefits administered by the states, as AFDC used to be, and Medicaid remains.

Both federal and state programs must comply with constitutional standards in setting eligibility rules and procedures for applying them. More information on state programs may be obtained by contacting the appropriate state agency that administers social services programs.

A directory of State Human Services Administrators is set forth at Appendix 1.

CHAPTER 2:
A PROFILE OF POVERTY IN AMERICA

POVERTY DEFINED

In general, the official definition of "poverty" considers a family's money income, before taxes, excluding capital gains and noncash benefits a family may receive, such as public housing, Medicaid, and food stamps. There are two slightly different versions of the federal poverty measure: (i) the poverty thresholds; and (ii) the poverty guidelines.

The Poverty Threshold

The poverty threshold is the first version of the federal poverty measure, originally developed by the Social Security Administration. Currently, it is the responsibility of the U.S. Census Bureau to determine who is poor. A set of money income thresholds, that vary by family size and composition, are used to make this assessment. If a family's total income is less than that family's threshold, then that family, and every individual in it, is considered poor.

The Census Bureau updates the poverty thresholds annually for inflation using the Consumer Price Index. The poverty thresholds do not vary geographically, and are used mainly for statistical purposes, such as preparing estimates of the number of Americans in poverty each year.

The Poverty Guidelines

The poverty guidelines—sometimes referred to as the "federal poverty level," are the alternate version of the federal poverty measure. They are issued each year by the Department of Health and Human Services and published in the Federal Register. The guidelines are a simplification of the poverty thresholds and used for administrative purposes, such as in determining financial eligibility for certain federal programs. The poverty guidelines are designated by the year in which they are issued. For example, the guidelines issued in February 2002 are designated the 2002 poverty guidelines.

In 1966, the United States established different poverty guidelines for Alaska and Hawaii from those established for the contiguous states. However, Puerto Rico and the United States territories do not have separately defined poverty guidelines. Thus, in cases in which a Federal program using the poverty guidelines serves any of those jurisdictions, the Federal office which administers the program is responsible for deciding whether to use the contiguous states' guidelines for those jurisdictions or to follow some other guidelines.

Programs using the guidelines in determining eligibility include Head Start, the Food Stamp Program, the National School Lunch Program, the Low-Income Home Energy Assistance Program, and the Children's Health Insurance Program. The cash public assistance programs, e.g., Temporary Assistance for Needy Families (TANF), and Supplemental Security Income (SSI) do not use the poverty guidelines in determining eligibility.

The Department of Health and Human Resources Poverty Guidelines for 2002 are set forth at Appendix 2.

THE DEMOGRAPHICS OF POVERTY

The poverty rate in the United States dropped to 11.3% in 2000, down half a percentage point from 1999. Although this rate was not statistically different from the record low of 11.1% set in 1973, it was lower than the rate for every year since, thus making the 2000 poverty rate the lowest in 21 years.

About 31.1 million people were considered "poor" in 2000—1.1 million fewer than in 1999. Many of the groups with poverty rates which declined between 1999 and 2000 historically have had high poverty rates. Most of the net decline in the overall poverty rate occurred among children, and individuals 18 to 24 years old.

Several groups set record low poverty rates in 2000, while the rates for others were not significantly different from their record lows:

Regional Differences

The decrease in poverty between 1999 and 2000 was not concentrated in any one region of the United States. The poverty rates in 2000 were 10.3% for the Northeast, 9.5% for the Midwest, 12.5% for the South, and 11.9% for the West. Since 1994, the South 's poverty rate has not been significantly different from that of the West. Prior to 1994, the South had the highest poverty rate among the four regions.

The poverty rate did fall significantly, from 8.3% in 1999 to 7.8% in 2000, for those living in the suburbs—i.e., metropolitan areas outside of central cities. For people living inside central cities, the poverty rate was 16.1 percent in 2000, statistically unchanged from 1999. Taking suburbs and central cities together, the poverty rate for people in metropolitan areas was 10.8 percent in 2000, down from 11.2 percent in 1999.

Among those individuals living outside metropolitan areas, the number of poor dropped to 6.8 million in 2000, down from 7.4 million in 1999. However, that decline did not translate to a lower poverty rate because 13.4 percent were poor in 2000, which is statistically unchanged from 1999.

Minority Groups

At 22.1%, African-Americans had their lowest measured poverty rates in 2000—down from 23.6% in 1999. The poverty rates for Hispanics, at 21.2%, was down from 22.8% in 1999, and the rates for Asians and Pacific Islanders at 10.8 percent, and White non-Hispanics, at 7.5%, were not statistically different from their measured lows.

While African-Americans remained disproportionately poor, the difference in poverty rates between African-Americans and White non-Hispanics narrowed since the most recent poverty rate peak. In 1993,the African-American poverty rate was 23.2 percentage points higher than that for White non-Hispanics. By 2000. this difference had fallen to 14.6 percentage points. Nevertheless, as in previous years, most of the poor in 2000 were White, at 68%, 47% of whom were White non-Hispanic.

Between 1999 and 2000, the foreign-born population, which includes both naturalized citizens and noncitizens, experienced no significant change in its poverty rate, at 15.7%, or in its number of poor, at 4.7 million. Among naturalized citizens, 1.1 million were poor in 2000, for a poverty rate of 9.7%. Among noncitizens, 3.6 million or 19.4 percent were poor in 2000, statistically unchanged from 1999.

Age

In 2000, the poverty rates for people 65 years old and over, at 10.2%, were not statistically different from their measured lows, although the number of poor elderly increased slightly from 3.2 million to 3.4 million from 1999. During the same time period, the poverty rate declined more for 18 to 24-year-olds than for any other age group, with a 3% drop from 17.3% to 14.4%. People age 18 to 64 had a poverty rate of 9.4% in 2000, down 0.6 percentage points from their 1999 rate of 10%.

The poverty rate for people under 18 years old dropped to 16.2 percent in 2000—down from 16.9 percent in 1999—which is this group's lowest poverty rate since 1979. Nevertheless, despite the decrease in child poverty, children under age 18 continued to have a higher poverty rate than other age groups.

Family Composition

Families with female heads of household, at 24.7%, had their lowest measured poverty rates in 2000 while married-couple families, at 4.7%, had poverty rates that were not statistically different from their measured lows.

Compared with the most recent poverty rate peak in 1993, a greater percentage of people in 2000 lived in families with at least one worker, and the poverty rate for people in these families fell since 1993. However, poor family members in 2000 were more likely to be living with at least one worker.

THE DEPTH OF POVERTY MEASUREMENTS

"Depth of poverty" refers to how much below the poverty threshold a family's income falls. The percentage of people whose family income was less than half their poverty threshold dropped significantly, from 4.6 percent in 1999 to 4.4 percent in 2000. Nevertheless, the number of people whose income fell below the 50th percentile of poverty remained statistically unchanged at 12.2 million in 2000. As in 1999, these people made up 39% of the poor population.

The so-called "near poor"—i.e., those with family incomes at least as great as their poverty threshold but less than 1.25 times their threshold—had no change in their number, at 12.3 million, or in their share, at 4.5%, of the total population in 2000.

Among people aged 65 and over, 2.2% were below 50 percent of their poverty threshold, compared with 4.4 percent for all people. However, among those below 125 percent of poverty, the elderly rate, at 16.9%, was higher than that for all people, at 15.8%. These differences indicate that people aged 65 and over were more highly concentrated just above the poverty level than they were among the extremely poor.

CHAPTER 3:
THE PERSONAL RESPONSIBILITY AND WORK OPPORTUNITY RECONCILIATION ACT OF 1996 (PRWORA)

THE PERSONAL RESPONSIBILITY AND WORK OPPORTUNITY RECONCILIATION ACT OF 1996

In August 1996, Congress enacted the Personal Responsibility and Work Opportunity Reconciliation Act (PRWORA), a comprehensive welfare reform law. The Act consists of nine "Titles," each of which are discussed in this Chapter and expanded upon elsewhere in this almanac.

The PRWORA Table of Contents is set forth at Appendix 3.

A major goal of the Act is to break the cycle of dependency on public assistance, and afford individuals the opportunity to obtain education and training to assist them in entering the workforce and becoming productive members of society. To this end, the Act requires work in exchange for time-limited public assistance, and provides support for families moving from welfare to work. Under the Act's provisions, by the year 2002, at least half of all welfare families and 90 percent of two-parent families must be in work activities.

In addition to the work requirements, the Act contains support provisions for families moving from welfare to work, including increased funding for child care and continued eligibility for medical coverage. The Act also strengthened the Child Support Enforcement Program, and made significant changes to the Food Stamp Program, and SSI Program for children, and placed restrictions on benefits available to legal immigrants. Modifications to the child nutrition program and reductions in the Social Services Block Grant are also provisions included in the Act.

Initial statistics demonstrate that the Act has been successful in decreasing the number of welfare recipients. Between its enactment in August 1996 and December 2001, the welfare caseload fell nearly 57 percent from 12.2 million recipients to fewer than 5.3 million. This is the largest welfare caseload decline in history and the lowest percentage of the population on welfare since 1965.

The legislation is due to be reauthorized by October 2002. The reauthorization proposal builds upon the apparent success of the welfare reform measures under the Act, and proposes further steps to assist welfare recipients achieve independence through work, protect children and strengthen families, and encourage state innovation in achieving these goals.

TITLE I: TEMPORARY ASSISTANCE TO NEEDY FAMILIES (TANF)

The PRWORA established the Temporary Assistance for Needy Families (TANF) program, which replaced the Aid to Families with Dependent Children (AFDC), Emergency Assistance (EA), and Job Opportunities and Basic Skills Training (JOBS) programs, and marked the end of federal entitlement to assistance. Under TANF, states and territories operate programs, and tribes have the option to run their own programs.

The Title I TANF Block Grant

Under the Act, states, territories, and tribes each receive a block grant allocation. The grant amount covers benefits, administrative expenses, and services targeted to needy families. The Act provides for an annual cost-sharing requirement placed upon the states, referred to as "maintenance of effort." Every fiscal year each state must spend a certain minimum amount of its own money to help eligible families in ways that are consistent with the purposes of the TANF program. The required amount is based on an "applicable percentage" of the state's prior expenditures on AFDC and the AFDC-related programs.

The Act offers states great flexibility in designing individual state TANF programs. Unless expressly provided under the statute, the federal government may not regulate the conduct of states. States may use the TANF funds in any manner "reasonably calculated to accomplish the purposes of TANF."

The stated purposes of TANF are: (i) assisting needy families so that children can be cared for in their own homes; (ii) reducing dependency of needy parents by promoting job preparation, work, and marriage; (iii) preventing out-of-wedlock pregnancies; and (iv) encouraging the formation and maintenance of two-parent families.

The findings of Congress in enacting Title I of the PRWORA establishing TANF is set forth at Appendix 3.

TANF grants and state maintenance of effort funds must be spent on families that include a child or expectant mother. In addition, there are restrictions on the use of federal funds, as follows:

(1) Assistance cannot be provided to families who have already received assistance under the programs for a cumulative total of 60 months. Notwithstanding this provision, in any one year, states can exempt up to 20% of their caseload from this five-year time limit. On the other hand, states can also set time limits that are shorter than five years.

(2) Unmarried teen parents must stay in school and live at home or in an adult-supervised setting.

(3) Persons who have been convicted of a drug-related felony are banned for life from TANF and the Food Stamp Program, although states can opt out of the ban or limit it.

(4) Persons who do not cooperate with child support enforcement requirements, including paternity establishment, receive a reduced benefit or may lose it entirely.

(5) No more than 15 percent of a state's TANF grant may be used for administrative costs.

State funds which are a part of the federal TANF program are not subject to the above restrictions, except for the child support enforcement requirements.

States can also supplement their block grant funding. This includes: (i) a $2 billion contingency fund over five years for states experiencing economic downturns; (ii) an $800 million fund over four years to provide supplemental grants for states with high population growth and low welfare spending; (iii) a $1.7 billion federal loan fund; (iv) a $1 billion appropriation over five years to make performance bonuses; and (v) a $100 million annual appropriation for bonuses to states that reduce the number of out-of-wedlock births and abortions.

Under the Act, states may be penalized if they fail to comply with any of the provisions. For example, a state's block grant may be reduced if the state fails to: (i) satisfy the work participation rate schedule; (ii) comply with five-year limit on assistance; (iii) meet the state's basic maintenance of effort requirements; (iv) meet the state's contingency fund requirement; (v) reduce recipient grants for refusing to participate in work activities without good cause; (vi) maintain assistance when a single custodial parent with a child under six cannot obtain child care; (vii) submit required data reports; (viii) comply with paternity establishment and child support enforcement requirements; (ix) participate in the Income and Eligibility Verification System; (x) repay a federal loan on time; (xi) use federal funds appropriately; or (xii) replace federal penalty reductions with additional state funds.

The total penalty assessed against a state in a given year may not exceed 25 percent of a state's block grant allotment. In some situations, states may avoid penalties: (1) if they demonstrate that they had reasonable cause for failing to meet the program requirements; or (2) if they develop a corrective compliance plan, receive approval of their plan, and correct or discontinue the violation.

Specific TANF Provisions

TANF includes a wide range of provisions designed to assist individuals who are making the transition from welfare to work, as further discussed below.

Work Requirements

Under the Act, welfare recipients must work after two years on assistance, with few exceptions. The welfare recipient's job qualifications and employment-readiness needs are assessed. To count toward state work requirements, recipients are required to participate in unsubsidized or subsidized employment, on-the-job training, work experience, community service, 12 months of vocational training, or to provide child care services to individuals who are participating in community service. Up to 6 weeks of job search can also count toward the work requirement. Single parents with a child under 6 who cannot find child care cannot be penalized for failure to meet the work requirements. A state may also exempt single parents with children under the age of one from the work requirements.

A directory of U.S. Department of Labor Welfare to Work Programs is set forth at Appendix 4.

Under the Act, a work participation rate schedule was established for the states to follow, which gradually increased since 1997. By 2002, states were required to have 50 percent of all families engaged in a work activity for a minimum of 30 hours per week, and 90 percent of two-parent families engaged in work activity for at least 35 hours per week.

The state work participation rate requirements for 1997 through 2002 are set forth at Appendix 5.

Child Care

Since the Act was enacted, more than $39 billion in federal funds have supported the child care needs of families transitioning from welfare to work. During the same time period, states have provided more than $11 billion as a part of their commitment to child care.

Health Care Coverage

The Act also guaranteed that individuals who meet pre-reform welfare-eligibility criteria will continue to be eligible to receive Medicaid, including at least six months of transitional Medicaid coverage when they leave welfare for work. In addition, the State Children's Health Insurance Program (SCHIP) provides health insurance coverage for uninsured children, many of whom come from working families with incomes too high to qualify for Medicaid but too low to afford private health insurance.

Five Year Time Limit

Under the Act, families with adult recipients who have received assistance for five cumulative years are ineligible for federally funded cash assistance. States have the option of setting a shorter time limit. States also are permitted to provide extensions after reaching the federal time limit to 20 percent of their caseload, and states have the option to provide continued support to families that reach the time limit using Social Services Block Grant or state funds.

Non-Custodial Parents

In an effort to strengthen the family structure, and promote two-parent families, the Act also provides services to non-custodial parents so that they are better able to support their children. The Act authorizes grants to help states establish programs that support and facilitate non-custodial parents' visitation with their children.

Teen Pregnancy

A major goal of the Act is to prevent teenage pregnancy and fund abstinence education activities for adolescents. In addition, unmarried minor parents must participate in educational and training activities and live with a responsible adult or in an adult-supervised setting in order to receive assistance. States are responsible for assisting in locating adult-supervised settings for teens who cannot live at home.

Child Support Enforcement

The Act also includes strong child support enforcement measures. Under the Act, each state is required to operate a child support enforcement program that meets federal requirements to be eligible for TANF block grants.

Paternity Establishment

The Act also streamlines the legal process for paternity establishment, making it easier and faster to establish paternity, and expands the voluntary in-hospital paternity establishment program. The Act also requires a state form for voluntary paternity acknowledgment, and requires the states to publicize the availability, and encourage the use, of voluntary paternity establishment processes. Under the Act, welfare recipients who fail to cooperate with paternity establishment will have their monthly cash assistance reduced by at least 25 percent. In 2000, paternity establishments rose to nearly 1.6 million, an increase of 12 percent from fiscal year 1999.

Refugee Assistance

Refugee assistance programs were established by the 1980 Immigration and Nationality Act in order to assist refugees in becoming employed, economically self-sufficient, and assimilated into American society as soon as possible after their arrival. The Act continues this goal by providing federal funds to states and non-profit organizations to help offset the costs of resettlement. Increasing refugee employment and reducing their dependency on welfare is a major emphasis of the Act.

Welfare to Work Grants

To assist those most at risk of long-term welfare dependency into jobs, the Balanced Budget Act of 1997 authorized a total of $3 billion over two years in Welfare-to-Work grants specifically focused on transitioning long-term welfare recipients into jobs. The grants target those in the welfare population who have the most significant barriers to employment, and are designed to help this group acquire the skills, work experience, and resources they need to find and keep permanent unsubsidized employment.

The U.S. Department of Labor is designated as the agency to oversee distribution of the grants. Seventy-five percent of funds authorized for distribution consist of formula grants to states, based on poverty rates and the number of welfare recipients in the state.

The balance of the authorized funds consist of competitive grants to local communities, which are awarded directly by the U.S. Department of Labor to local governments, Private Industry Councils, and qualified private organizations. The competitive grants fund projects that are designed to transition welfare recipients who are least job ready into unsubsidized employment. These grants are targeted to urban and rural areas with large concentrations of poverty.

Welfare to Work Programs and Substance Abuse

The connection between unemployment and substance abuse creates a vicious cycle with one exacerbating the other. In today's labor force, 16% of the unemployed report current illicit drug use and 9.1% of the unemployed report heavy alcohol use. The prevalence of substance abuse problems among welfare recipients is unknown, but estimates vary from 6.6% to 37%.

The Act recognizes that intervention is needed to help those who are recovering from addiction to be able to find and retain employment. However, many individuals who require such intervention, and are in the welfare system, fear that admitting their addiction will jeopardize their eligibility for benefits and cause them to lose custody of their children.

The welfare-to-work program has identified the need for substance abuse treatment as one eligibility factor and recognizes non-medical treatment as an example of an allowable job retention service. Under the Act, using federal funds for non-medical substance abuse treatment is permissible since it addresses the need of a particular target group and can help individuals make successful transitions to work. Many American workplaces now have programs specifically designed to address workplace drug abuse, which have proven particularly helpful to the welfare recipient who is recovering from a substance abuse problem.

TITLE II: SUPPLEMENTAL SECURITY INCOME (SSI)

The Act changed the definition of disability for children that requires a child, in order to be eligible for SSI benefits, to have a specific medically determinable physical or mental impairment which results in "marked and severe" functional limitations and which can be expected to last for at least 12 months or to result in death. The Social Security Administration (SSA) is required to remove the references to "maladaptive behavior" as a medical criterion for evaluating mental disabilities in children.

The new definition applies immediately to new claims for assistance, including claims that have not been finally adjudicated as of the date of enactment. The SSA was required to redetermine the cases of children who were currently receiving SSI to determine whether they met the new criteria. The SSA appeals process is available to individuals who are found ineligible.

The SSI program is discussed more fully in Chapter 4 of this almanac.

TITLE III: CHILD SUPPORT PROVISIONS

In order to receive the TANF block grant, states must operate a child support enforcement program. Applicants for and recipients of TANF assistance and Medicaid must assign support rights to the state and cooperate with child support enforcement efforts. Failure to cooperate with such efforts without good cause may cause a family to lose its cash assistance or be penalized a minimum of 25 percent from their cash assistance grant. States that fail to do so will be penalized up to 5 percent of the TANF block grant in the next fiscal year.

TITLE IV: RESTRICTING WELFARE AND PUBLIC BENEFITS FOR ALIENS

Under the Act, most legal immigrants were no longer considered eligible for SSI or the Food Stamp Program. However, recent legislation enacted in 2002 has eased the restrictions on food stamp eligibility requirements for legal immigrants and noncitizens.

Aside from the SSI program and the food stamp program, states have the authority to decide whether or not qualified aliens will be eligible for Medicaid, the Temporary Assistance for Needy Families (TANF) block grant, and the Social Services Block Grant (SSBG).

States may not deny assistance to certain legal immigrants, including refugees during their first 5 years in the U.S., asylees and persons whose deportation has been withheld for 5 years from the date they received such status, permanent residents who have worked in the United States long enough to qualify for social security coverage, and veterans or active duty military service personnel or their spouses or unmarried dependent children.

TITLE V: CHILD PROTECTION

Under the Act, most provisions of prior law regarding child protection are retained. States are required to use the AFDC rules and requirements in effect as of June 1, 1995, under their state plan to determine eligibility for child protective services under Title IV-E. The law allows states to use IV-E dollars to pay for-profit providers to care for children in foster care, and requires states to give preference to relatives when deciding upon foster care placements, provided that the relative care-giver meets all relevant state child protection standards.

TITLE VI: CHILD CARE

The Act consolidates previous child care funding sources with the Child Care and Development Block Grant. States automatically get about $1.2 billion in "mandatory" funds, and appropriated "discretionary" funds authorized at $1 billion each year. Under the Act, the previous individual entitlements to child care for AFDC recipients and former recipients who have left AFDC for work are eliminated. Nevertheless, states may not penalize single parents with children under 6 who cannot find child care for failure to participate in work activities.

TITLE VII: CHILD NUTRITION PROGRAMS

The Act established a two-tier system of reimbursements under the Child and Adult Care Food Program. The current rates for family or group day care homes located in areas in which at least 50 percent of the children are in households that are below 185 percent of the poverty level, or are operated by a provider whose income is below 185 percent of the poverty level, were continued. Other homes receive reduced meal reimbursements. The Act also reduced the maximum reimbursement rates in the Summer Food Service Program and for full-price meals in the school breakfast and school lunch programs and in child care centers.

TITLE VIII: FOOD STAMPS AND COMMODITY DISTRIBUTION

The Act sets maximum food stamp benefit levels at 100% of the Thrifty Food Plan. In addition, able-bodied recipients age 18-50 with no dependents must be engaged in work or work programs in order to be eligible for food stamps. Otherwise, their eligibility is limited to 3 months in any 36-month period. Recipients who find work and then lose their job may receive up to 3 additional months of benefits. Work programs include job training and workfare, but not job search or job readiness programs.

Further, states are authorized to operate a "simplified Food Stamp Program" for households that include individuals receiving assistance under TANF. The simplified program allows for a single set of rules to determine eligibility and benefits. Such a program may not increase federal costs above what they would have been under the regular program. States may disqualify food stamp recipients who fail to cooperate with child support enforcement or who are delinquent in paying child support.

TITLE IX: MISCELLANEOUS

Teen Pregnancy Reduction

Under the Act, the U.S. Department of Health and Human Services (HHS) is required to develop and implement a national strategy to reduce the incidence of teenage pregnancy and, under TANF, HHS is also authorized to make annual bonus grants to the five states which reduce all out-of-wedlock births by the greatest amount, without increasing the abortion rate.

Social Services Block Grants

The Act set funding for the Social Services Block Grant (SSBG) at $2.38 billion in 1996-2002, and $2.8 billion in 2003 and thereafter. Non-cash vouchers for children that become ineligible for cash assistance under TANF time limits are authorized as an allowable use of the Social Security Block Grant funds.

CHAPTER 4:
SUPPLEMENTAL SECURITY INCOME

DEVELOPMENT OF THE SUPPLEMENTAL SECURITY INCOME PROGRAM

As set forth in Chapter 1, the Social Security Act of 1935 established programs for needy elderly, blind and disabled individuals. These three programs were known as the "adult categories," and were initially administered by state and local governments with partial federal funding. Over the years, the state programs became more complex, and payments were inconsistent among the states. For example, payments varied more than 300% from state to state.

Due to this disparity, the federal government recognized a need to reform these programs and, in 1971, it was proposed that the Social Security Administration (SSA) administer the "adult categories" because of its reputation for successful administration of the existing social insurance programs. In 1972, the Social Security Amendment was passed, and Congress federalized the "adult categories" by creating the Supplemental Security Income (SSI) program.

SSI has evolved into a federal welfare program for adults and children who are disabled or blind, and people aged 65 and over with low income and few financial resources. General tax revenues from the U.S. Treasury are used to finance the SSI program.

ELIGIBILITY

In order to be eligible for SSI payments, one's income and assets must fall below certain established limits. Not all assets are taken into account. For example, a home and personal belongings are not counted, but bank accounts and cash on hand are included in the calculation. In addition, although eligibility for SSI would not be affected by the ability of one's children to support them, any support actually received from one's children would be considered income for SSI purposes and could affect the amount of one's payment.

Although SSI is a federal program, some states supplement the national payments and have established higher SSI rates and allow higher income limits than others. It is important, therefore, to ascertain your individual state's eligibility for the SSI program. Unlike the "income" limits, however, the SSI "asset" limits do not vary among the states.

You don't have to qualify for Social Security benefits in order to get SSI, and it is possible to get both Social Security and SSI. However, if you're applying based on a disability, you must meet the same standard for disability as with regular Social Security benefits.

BENEFITS

The SSI program provides a basic payment for an eligible individual and a larger amount for an eligible couple. The payment for a couple is lower than that made to two individuals because married people living together generally share expenses and live more economically than two people living independently.

People who qualify for SSI receive a check each month. The amount of benefit may vary depending on the recipient's state of residence and level of income. If you qualify for SSI, you are also automatically entitled to health care coverage under the Medicaid program. In addition, an SSI recipient may also be eligible for food stamps and other social services.

One can apply for SSI and Medicaid by completing forms provided by their local welfare office, department of social services or SSA office. If the application is approved, the recipient will be paid benefits based on the date the application was filed.

The SSA reviews every SSI case from time to time to make sure the individuals who are receiving checks are still eligible and entitled to receive benefits. The review also determines if the individuals are receiving the correct amounts.

RIGHT TO APPEAL AND REPRESENTATION

If the application for SSI benefits is not approved, the individual can appeal that decision. The procedure for appealing an SSI determination is similar to appealing for more Social Security benefits. An applicant has 60 days to submit a written request for reconsideration. The request should be sent to the local Social Security district office, and should state the reasons why the applicant disagrees with the determination. Depending on the nature of the issue, either a case review, a formal conference or a hearing may follow.

If the applicant does not appeal the determination within 60 days, their options are limited unless they can show there was a good reason for filing late. Without such a showing, the applicant may be able to file a new application and seek retroactive collection of benefits, or try to re-open the claim by filing a petition with a judge who is specially designated to hear Social Security appeals.

The applicant also has the right to designate a representative to act on his or her behalf in dealing with the SSA by filing an Appointment of Representative form (SSA Form 1696-U4). The representative must also accept the appointment by signing the form.

It is important to select an individual who is qualified to act in this capacity as the representative will have the authority to act on the applicant's behalf in most Social Security matters. Often, the appointee will be an attorney who is familiar with the Social Security system. An applicant does not need a lawyer to represent them on appeal, however, there are lawyers available who handle these type of cases. In addition, most legal services organizations will provide a lawyer free of charge to those unable to afford one. Once an appointment of representative is made and filed with the SSA, the SSA will deal directly with that individual on all matters affecting the applicant's Social Security claim.

If the representative will not be charging a fee for their services, they must also sign a waiver of fee. Representatives who intend to charge a fee must obtain approval from the SSA by filing a fee petition or fee agreement with the SSA.

WELFARE REFORM RESTRICTIONS

The welfare reform movement brought about significant changes in the SSI program. As set forth in Chapter 1, the passage of the Contract with America Advancement Act of 1996 narrowed the number of people allowed to receive SSI disability benefits by requiring that drug addiction or alcoholism not be a material factor in their disability. Another significant change was the complete exclusion of legal aliens from receiving any SSI benefits.

CHAPTER 5:
THE FOOD STAMP PROGRAM

IN GENERAL

In 1964, Congress passed the Food Stamp Act, which established the most significant federally funded food plan in the United States. The mission of the Food Stamp Program is to end hunger and improve the nutrition and health of low income adults and children. The program is in operation in the 50 States, the District of Columbia, Guam and the U.S. Virgin Islands.

Individuals who work for low wages, are unemployed or work part-time, receive public assistance, are elderly or disabled and have a small income, or are homeless may be eligible for food stamps. The federal government pays for the amount of the benefit received. State public assistance agencies are responsible for administering the program, and fund the costs of determining eligibility and distributing the food stamps.

The Food Stamp Program provides food "stamps," in the form of paper coupons or electronic benefits on debit cards, for needy individuals that can be exchanged like money at authorized retail food stores. Food stamps can only be used for food items and for plants and seeds used to grow food. Food stamps cannot be used to purchase nonfood items.

Selected provisions of the Food Stamp Act are set forth at Appendix 6.

THE APPLICATION PROCESS

An application for food stamps may be obtained in person at a local food stamp office, over the phone, or by mail. Applicants who are also applying for or receiving Supplemental Security Income (SSI) benefits may apply for food stamps at their local Social Security Administration office. In addition, households that are applying for public assistance can apply for food stamps at the same time.

The food stamp office will accept the application on the same day it is received. Individuals who have difficulty filling out the application form can obtain assistance from a food stamp worker. All questions must be answered completely and honestly or the applicant can be removed from the program, and face fines and/or imprisonment. After the application has been submitted, the food stamp office will contact the applicant to set up an interview to go over the application.

During the interview, the food stamp worker will explain the program rules and will require proof of certain information contained on the application. If the applicant has trouble obtaining documentation needed, the food stamp worker may be able to assist the applicant in the process.

Some of the documentation the applicant may need to produce includes: (i) proof of citizenship or status as an eligible non-citizen; (ii) social security number for every member of the household, including children; (iii) proof of income; and (iv) proof of compliance with the work rules.

A directory of Food Stamp Program information numbers, by state, is set forth at Appendix 7.

ELIGIBILITY

To be eligible to receive food stamps, a household must meet certain eligibility standards, as set forth below.

Assets and Resources

Under the food stamp eligibility rules, the applicant's assets and resources, such as bank accounts, cash, real estate, personal property, vehicles, etc., are considered in determining whether a household is eligible to get food stamps. Some resources are counted toward the allowable limit and some are not.

All households may have up to $2,000 worth of countable resources and still be eligible. Households may have up to $3,000 and still be eligible if at least one member is age 60 or older. The resources of people who get public assistance, SSI, and, in some locations, general assistance are not counted toward the limit.

Some assets and resources that will not be counted are the applicant's: (i) home and surrounding lot; (ii) household goods and personal belongings; and (iii) life insurance policies.

Examples of resources that will be counted are the applicant's: (i) cash and funds in checking and savings accounts; (ii) stocks and bonds; and (iii) land and buildings, other than the applicant's home and lot, that do not produce income.

Vehicles

A vehicle is not counted as a resource if it is (i) used for producing income for the household; (ii) annually producing income consistent with its fair market value; (iii) necessary for long-distance travel for work other than daily commuting; (iv) used as the household's home; (v) necessary to transport a physically disabled household member; (vi) needed to carry most of the household's fuel or water; or (vii) if the household has little equity in the vehicle because of money owed on the vehicle, or because it would bring no more than the statutory dollar amount, if sold.

For the following vehicles, the fair market value is determined, and any amount over the statutory dollar amount, is a resource that will be counted: (i) one vehicle per adult household member; and (ii) any other vehicle a teen-aged member of the household drives to work, school, job training or to look for work.

For all other vehicles, the fair market value over the statutory amount, or the equity value—i.e., the market value of the vehicle less the amount the household owes on it—whichever is more, is a resource that will be counted.

Income

Under the food stamp rules, almost all types of income are counted to determine if a household is eligible. Most households must have income at or below certain dollar limits before and after deductions are allowed. However, households in which all members are getting public assistance or SSI do not have to meet the income eligibility tests.

The applicant will be required to provide proof of the income of all household members. Examples of proof may include the employee's latest pay stubs; an employer's statement; and/or benefit letters from Social Security, Veterans Administration, unemployment compensation, or employee pensions funds.

The most recent Food Stamp Program Income Eligibility Guidelines are set forth at Appendix 8.

Income Deductions

After adding all of the household's countable income, the food stamp worker will subtract certain deductions. The income after deductions must fall below a certain dollar amount for the household to get food stamps. This dollar amount will depend on the number of people in the household.

The following deductions are allowed for all households:

1. A standard statutory deduction.

2. Twenty percent of earned income.

3. Actual costs of dependent care. There is a dollar limit on the amount of this deduction. Dependent care includes care for children and disabled adults if this care is needed so that a household member can work, look for a job, or get training or education leading to a job.

4. Legally owed child-support payments.

5. Shelter expenses that are more than half of the household's income. There is a dollar limit on the amount of shelter expenses that may be deducted unless there is an elderly or disabled member. If there is an elderly or disabled member, the dollar limit does not apply.

6. Medical expenses over $35 a month for household members who are age 60 or older or receiving certain disability payments. However, medical costs are deductible only if they are not covered by insurance, a government program, or some other source.

The applicant will be required to provide proof of certain deductible expenses, such as proof of (i) dependent-care costs; (ii) child-support payments, e.g., a court order and canceled checks; (iii) rent or mortgage; (iv) homeowner insurance; (v) utilities, e.g., telephone, electricity, gas, oil, water, sewerage, garbage collection, and installation costs for utilities; and (vi) medical expenses and proof of any reimbursement, such as an insurance policy or statement from an insurance company or agency paying these bills.

Work Requirements

Able-bodied adults between 16 and 60 must register for work, take part in an employment and training program to which they are referred by the food stamp office, and accept or continue suitable employment. Failure to comply with these requirements can result in disqualification from the Food Stamp Program.

In addition, able-bodied adults between 18 and 50 who do not have any dependent children and are not pregnant are only eligible for food stamps for 3 months in a 36-month period if they do not work or participate in a workfare or employment and training program other than job search. Nevertheless, other members of the household may continue to get food stamps even if this person is disqualified.

There are some limited exceptions to the work rules. For example, a single parent enrolled full time in college and taking care of a dependent household member under the age of 12 can generally qualify for food stamps if otherwise eligible.

BENEFITS

Once an individual is deemed eligible for food stamps, they are generally sent to the recipient no later than 30 days from the date the application was received by the food stamp office. In particularly urgent situations, a household may be able to obtain food stamps within 7 days.

The food stamp benefit amount is based on the U.S. Department of Agriculture's Thrifty Food Plan, which is an estimate of how much it costs to buy food to prepare nutritious, low-cost meals for a household. This estimate is changed every year to keep pace with food prices.

The amount of food stamps an eligible household receives depends on the number of people in the household and the amount of household income. In calculating the household's food stamp benefit—referred to as their allotment—households with income are expected to use about 30 percent of their own money for food, after certain deduction have been allowed.

The most recent maximum monthly food stamp allotment chart, by size of household, is set forth at Appendix 9.

SPECIAL RULES FOR THE ELDERLY AND DISABLED

For purposes of the Food Stamp Program, a person is considered elderly if he or she is 60 years of age or older. A person is considered disabled if he or she:

1. Receives Federal disability or blindness payments under the Social Security Act, including Supplemental Security Income (SSI) or Social Security disability or blindness payments;

2. Receives State disability or blindness payments based on SSI rules;

3. Receives a disability retirement benefit from a governmental agency because of a disability considered permanent under the Social Security Act;

4. Receives an annuity under the Railroad Retirement Act and is eligible for Medicare or is considered to be disabled based on the SSI rules;

5. Is a veteran who is totally disabled, permanently housebound, or in need of regular aid and attendance; or

6. Is a surviving spouse or child of a veteran who is receiving VA benefits and is considered to be permanently disabled.

If a person cannot apply for food stamps personally, an authorized representative may apply and attend the interview on their behalf. If nobody is available to represent the applicant, the office interview may be waived, and the food stamp office will interview the applicant by telephone or a home visit.

Although a household is generally considered to include everyone who lives together and purchases and prepares meals together, if a person is 60 years of age or older and he or she is unable to purchase and prepare meals separately because of a permanent disability, the person and the person's spouse may be a separate household, for the purposes of food stamp eligibility, if the others they live with do not have very much income.

In addition, people are not normally eligible for food stamps if they receive their meals in an institutional setting. However, an exception exists for elderly and disabled persons, as follows:

1. Residents of federally subsidized housing for the elderly may be eligible for food stamps, even though they receive their meals at the facility.

2. Disabled persons who live in certain nonprofit group living arrangements may be eligible for food stamps, even though the group home prepares their meals for them.

In addition, a household with an elderly member may have up to $3,000 in resources whereas a household without an elderly person may only have up to $2000 in resources. Further, if a vehicle is needed to transport a physically disabled household member, its value is not counted.

In order to be eligible for food stamps, most households have to meet both a monthly gross income test and a monthly net income test. However, households in which all members are receiving SSI or TANF are considered to be eligible based on income, and households with one or more elderly members only have to meet the net income test, which is gross income minus certain deductions.

THE ELECTRONIC BENEFITS TRANSFER SYSTEM

In most states today, food stamp benefits are delivered electronically to Electronic Benefits Transfer (EBT) accounts. Soon, all benefits will be delivered by EBT systems. Under this system, the recipient receives a plastic card with a magnetic strip, similar to a credit or debit card, to access their food stamp EBT account at authorized food retail outlets.

Along with the EBT card, the recipient receives a Personal Identification Number (PIN) that protects their benefits from unauthorized use by another. The PIN is a secret number, known only to the recipient, that allows them to use the EBT card to purchase eligible food items. The PIN number should be kept separate from the EBT card so that it is not stolen. Without the PIN, nobody else can use the EBT card.

Most states mail the EBT cards to the recipients, along with instructions on its use. If the EBT card is mailed, the recipient will receive their PIN in the mail several days after receiving the EBT card. If the state delivers EBT cards over-the-counter, the recipient's local case worker will explain the process for receiving the EBT card and PIN, and provide training on use of the card.

Food stamp benefits are automatically deposited into the food stamp EBT account once the applicant is determined to be eligible to receive food stamp benefits. For every month of eligibility, food stamp benefits are automatically deposited into the EBT account.

The recipient uses the EBT card at authorized food retail stores just as he or she would use a credit or debit card. However, the EBT card can only be used for eligible food items. Ineligible items include: (i) pet foods; (ii) soaps; (iii) paper products; (iv) household supplies; (v) grooming items, such as toothpaste, and cosmetics; (vi) alcoholic beverages and tobacco; (vii) vitamins and medicines; and (viii) hot foods and any food that will be eaten in the store.

The cost of the eligible food items purchased are subtracted from the amount in the food stamp EBT account, up to the remaining balance. The recipient will receive a receipt that shows the amount of their food stamp purchase and the amount of food stamp benefits remaining in their EBT account.

REPORTING REQUIREMENTS

Some households are required to periodically report on their household circumstances. Other households are required to report changes as they become known. It is important to report any changes so that the benefit amount is adjusted accordingly. If it is determined that a household has received more food stamps than they are eligible for due to a change in their circumstances, they may be required to pay back any difference.

THE APPLICANT'S RIGHTS AND RESPONSIBILITIES

Rights

An applicant for food stamps has certain rights in connection with their application, including the right to:

1. Receive an application, and have their application accepted on the same day that they go to the food stamp office;

2. Have an adult who knows the applicant's situation apply for them if they cannot get to the food stamp office;

3. Obtain their food stamps within 30 days after they apply if they qualify;

4. Obtain food stamps within 7 days if they are in immediate need and qualify for faster service;

5. Not be discriminated against because they are elderly or because of sex, race, color, disability, religious creed, national origin, or political beliefs;

6. Be told in advance if the food stamp office is going to reduce or end their benefits during their certification period because of a change in their situation that they did not report in writing;

7. Review their own case file and obtain a copy of the Food Stamp Program rules; and

8. Have a fair hearing if they don't think the rules were applied correctly in their case.

Responsibilities

The applicant for food stamps has certain responsibilities in connection with their application, including the following:

1. The applicant must answer all application questions completely and honestly, and sign their name to certify, under penalty of perjury, that all their answers are true.

2. The applicant must provide proof of their eligibility.

3. The applicant must promptly report changes in household circumstances to the food stamp office.

4. The applicant must not put their money or assets in another's name in order to qualify for food stamps.

5. The applicant must not make any changes on any food stamp cards or documents.

6. The applicant must not sell, trade, or give away their food stamps, or any food stamp cards or documents.

7. The applicant must use their food stamps only to buy eligible items.

Applicants who violate these rules may be disqualified from the food stamp program, and may face fines and/or imprisonment. Food stamp fraud, misuse, waste or abuse can be reported by calling 1-800-424-9121.

FAIR HEARINGS

If the application for food stamps is denied, the applicant will receive a notice explaining the denial. If the applicant believes the application was wrongly denied, or disagrees with the amount of food stamps allotted, the applicant should contact the food stamp office. If they maintain their position, the applicant is entitled to have the case reviewed at a fair hearing.

The applicant may request a fair hearing in writing, in person, or over the phone. A friend or relative may assist the applicant in preparing for the hearing, and may attend the hearing with the applicant.

If the hearing official decides in favor of the applicant, he or she will begin to get the correct amount of food stamps they are entitled to receive, including retroactive benefits.

THE WELFARE REFORM MOVEMENT

The Personal Responsibility and Work Opportunity Reconciliation Act of 1996 (PRWORA), more fully discussed in Chapter 3 of this almanac, substantially reduced the size of the Food Stamp Program. For example, the Act made adjustments in the "Thrifty Food Plan," a low-cost food budget used to calculate food stamp awards, and created time-limits for benefits to able-bodied adults without dependents.

Restrictions on Immigrants

Although the Act eliminated the food stamp benefits previously available to most legal immigrants, recent legislation has eased these restrictions. On May 13, 2002, President Bush signed the "Farm Security and Rural Investment Act of 2002" that will allow more low-income non-citizen and legal immigrants receive food stamps if they meet the Food Stamp Program's income and resource requirements.

Legal Immigrants

The PRWORA virtually eliminated food stamp benefits to legal immigrants. The 2002 law allows eligibility for legal immigrants who meet the program's requirements, and who:

1. Receive disability benefits, such as SSI or disability-related Medicaid;

2. Have lived in the United States for 5 years in a qualified status or are under 18 years old and entered the United States after Aug. 22, 1996.

Qualified immigrants include lawful permanent residents—i.e., holders of green cards; refugees; asylees; people granted withholding of deportation or removal; Cuban/Haitian entrants; individuals who have received INS parole in the United States for a least one year; conditional entrants; and certain victims of domestic violence.

Immigrants who are not eligible can still apply for their eligible children and eligible members of their household. However, the ineligible applicant will still have to show proof of their income and resources to determine the amount of food stamp benefits the eligible household members are entitled to receive.

Receiving food stamps does not make an immigrant a "public charge," therefore it does not hurt an immigrant's chance of becoming a citizen and he or she will not be deported, denied entry to the country, or denied permanent status or a "green card" because he or she receives food stamps.

In addition to federal benefits, individual states may offer food program assistance to legal immigrants.

A directory of states which offer food programs for legal immigrants, including eligibility dates and requirements, is set forth at Appendix 10.

Non-Citizens

Under the PRWORA, noncitizens who were eligible for food stamps, which included refugees, asylees and deportees, were only able to receive benefits for a period of 7 years after they entered the country or their status was granted.

Under the 2002 law, there is no longer a seven-year limit on food stamps for refugees, asylees, Amerasians, and Cuban or Haitian entrants. Beginning on April 1, 2003, these non-citizens will be eligible as long as they qualify for the program based on income and resources.

Certain other non-citizens eligible for food stamps include certain battered aliens, and individuals admitted for lawful permanent residence who have a military connection or who can be credited with 40 quarters of work.

In addition, refugees, asylees, deportees, battered aliens, and lawful permanent residents may also be eligible if they were lawfully living in the United States on August 22, 1996, and were over 65 on that date, are now under 18, or are receiving disability or blindness payments. The status of non-citizens must be verified.

ADDITIONAL GOVERNMENT-FUNDED FOOD PROGRAMS

In addition to the Food Stamp Program, the federal government also provides grants for other food programs, as set forth below.

The Child and Adult Care Food Program (CACFP)

The Child and Adult Care Food Program (CACFP) supplies federal grants of money and food to nonprofit elementary and secondary schools and to child-care institutions so that they can serve milk, well-balanced meals, and snacks to children. Its aim is to provide good nutrition to the country's children.

The Special Supplemental Food Program For Women, Infants and Children (WIC)

The Special Supplemental Food Program For Women, Infants and Children (WIC) provides food for pregnant and nursing women, as well as infants and children under five years old.

CHAPTER 6:
MEDICAID

IN GENERAL

The Medicaid program was established in 1965 as an amendment to the Social Security Act of 1935 and was administered by the Social Security Administration until 1977. In 1977, administration of the Medicaid program was transferred to the Department of Health and Human Services and to the Health Care Financing Administration. The Medicaid program continued to be administered by the Health Care Financing Administration until June 2001, when the agency was renamed the Centers for Medicare and Medicaid Services (CMS).

Medicaid is jointly financed and administered by the federal and state governments as the primary source of health care coverage for low-income individuals, as well as the blind, and disabled populations in America. Each state has its own rules concerning eligibility and coverage, which may be complex, therefore, the reader is advised to check the law of his or her own jurisdiction for specific rules. This chapter presents an overview of the Medicaid program.

ELIGIBILITY

In general, to be eligible for Medicaid, a person must fit into a Medicaid eligibility category. Once a person is determined to fit into a Medicaid eligible category, the applicant's financial situation is examined. The applicant's income and resources are analyzed using a formula involving exemptions and deductions to determine the applicant's "countable" income and resources.

The applicant's countable income is then compared to the income guideline set by the state—i.e., the maximum amount of income a person can have and still be eligible for Medicaid, and their countable resources are compared to the state's resources guideline. If the applicant's income is less than or equal to the guideline, the person is considered income-eligible. A similar analysis is made of the applicant's resources. If it is determined that the applicant is both income-eligible and resource-eligible, he or she is considered qualified for Medicaid benefits.

Federal Requirements

Although states have discretion in setting their own income and resources guidelines, in order to qualify for federal funds, the federal government requires the states to provide Medicaid coverage under certain circumstances to specified groups. For example, states are required to cover:

1. Low income families with children, as described in Section 1931 of the Social Security Act, who meet certain eligibility requirements;

2. Recipients of Supplemental Security Income (SSI), which generally includes the needy elderly, the blind and disabled;

3. Infants born to Medicaid-eligible pregnant women. In such cases, Medicaid eligibility must continue throughout the first year of the child's life provided the infant remains in the mother's household and the mother remains eligible, or would be eligible if she were still pregnant.

4. Children under age 6 and pregnant women whose family income is at or below 133 percent of the Federal poverty level. States are also required to extend Medicaid eligibility until age 19 to all children born after September 30, 1983 in families with incomes at or below the Federal poverty level.

5. Recipients of adoption assistance and foster care under Title IV-E of the Social Security Act;

6. Certain Medicare beneficiaries, as set forth below; and

7. Groups who may be eligible for Medicaid on a temporary basis, including: (i) individuals who lose SSI payments due to earnings from work or increased Social Security benefits; (ii) families who are provided 6 to 12 months of Medicaid coverage following loss of eligibility under Section 1931 due to earnings, or (iii) families who are provided 4 months of Medicaid coverage following loss of eligibility under Section 1931 due to an increase in child or spousal support.

THE MEDICARE/MEDICAID RELATIONSHIP

The Medicare program provides hospital insurance, known as Part A coverage, to persons aged 65 and older who have insured status under Social Security or Railroad Retirement. Supplementary medical insurance, known as Part B coverage, requires payment of monthly premiums.

Medicare recipients who have low income and limited resources may receive help paying their out-of-pocket medical expenses from their state's Medicaid program. This is generally referred to as "dual eligibility." Services that are covered by both programs are paid first by Medicare, and the difference is paid Medicaid, up to the state's designated limit.

Medicaid also covers additional services, such as prescription drugs, hearing aids, eyeglasses, and nursing facility care beyond the time period covered by Medicare.

In addition, Medicaid may make certain payments on behalf of qualified Medicare recipients. Qualified Medicare Beneficiaries with resources at or below twice the standard allowed under the SSI program, and income at or below 100% of the Federal poverty level, do not have to pay their monthly Medicare premiums, deductibles, and coinsurance. Specified Low-Income Medicare Beneficiaries with resources at or below twice the standard allowed under the SSI program and income exceeding the Qualified Medicare Beneficiary level, but less than 120% of the federal poverty level, do not have to pay the monthly Medicare Part B premiums.

THE MEDICALLY NEEDY

Although not mandatory, states may extend Medicaid eligibility to the "medically needy,"—i.e., individuals who may have too much income to qualify under the mandatory needy groups. This group is able to "spend down" to Medicaid eligibility by incurring medical expenses to offset their excess income, thereby reducing it to a level below the maximum allowed by the state's Medicaid plan. However, states may only offer medically needy coverage to the aged, blind, and disabled populations if they also offer it to pregnant women and children.

Spending Down

To illustrate the "spending down" requirement, assume the state's medically needy income level is set at $600 per month. If the medically needy individual has a monthly income of $800 per month, he or she must "spend down" $200 per month to be eligible for Medicaid benefits. The spend down amount is multiplied by the state's budget period—e.g. six months—to determine the total spend down requirement. Using the foregoing example, the applicant's total spend down requirement would be $1200 ($200 x 6 months). Once the individual's medical bills reach the total spend down requirement, he or she is then covered by the Medicaid program for the remainder of the budget period.

POVERTY LEVEL GROUPS

Under the Omnibus Budget Reconciliation Act of 1986, states were also given the option to extend benefits to all aged and disabled persons with incomes up to 100% of the federal poverty level. States are also free to apply less restrictive methods when determining how to count income and resources for this group.

LONG-TERM CARE

Congress recognized that, as the baby boomer generation approaches retirement age, a comprehensive and reliable system for providing long-term care will be imperative to meet the needs of this growing aging population. Medicaid is the primary public provider for home health and nursing home care. Medicaid covered 40 percent of long-term care expenses for the elderly in 2000.

Through Medicaid, states have substantial flexibility to provide home and community-based services as an alternative to institutional care. Medicaid supports approximately 260 state home and community-based service waivers that provide beneficiaries with alternatives to institutional care and enable seniors and people with disabilities to receive services at home.

The Special Income Rule

When long-term care is unavoidable, Congress gave states the option to use a special income rule to provide Medicaid to persons in institutions who have too much income to qualify for SSI benefits, but not enough income to cover their expensive long-term care. Under the special income rule, states may set a special income standard of up to 300% of the maximum SSI benefit.

The income standard applies to gross income only without exemptions or deductions. The resource standards are generally the same as those in the SSI program. In addition, the states must allow nursing facility residents to retain a small amount of their income as an allowance for personal items.

Spousal Impoverishment Provisions

Each state also has spousal impoverishment provisions which provide that when one spouse is institutionalized for at least 30 days, the other spouse, referred to as the "community spouse," does not lose all income and resources. In such a case, the community spouse's income is not considered available to the institutionalized spouse. The purpose of this rule is to protect the community spouse from becoming impoverished and in need of public assistance.

To determine the community spouse's share of resources, the couple's resources are combined and then divided in half to determine the spousal share. The spousal share is then compared to the state's community spouse protected resource amount (CSRA), and the amount actually protected for the community spouse is the greater of either the spousal share or the CSRA. The couple's home, household goods, automobile, and burial funds are not included in the calculation.

In setting a CSRA, the state may exceed the federally prescribed minimum, but may not exceed the federal maximum.

CHAPTER 7:
PROMOTING CHILD WELFARE

IN GENERAL

A number of programs designed to protect and promote the health and well-being of children have been established by the federal government and are administered by designated federal and state agencies under the auspices of the U.S. Department of Health and Human Services (HHS). Some of the most important programs are discussed below.

CHILD HEALTH

The State Children's Health Insurance Program (SCHIP)

The State Children's Health Insurance Program (SCHIP) is a program created under the Social Security Act that provides health insurance coverage to children whose families have incomes that are too high to qualify for Medicaid but too low to afford private health insurance. SCHIP is a partnership between the federal and state governments. Under the program, states may choose to expand their Medicaid programs, design a separate child health program, or use a combination of both.

States choosing separate child health programs must offer either the same or "equivalent" benefits as those offered under one of three benchmark plans: the standard Blue Cross/Blue Shield Preferred Provider Option offered by the Federal Employees Health Benefit Program; a health benefit plan offered by the state to its employees; or the HMO benefit plan with the largest commercial enrollment in the state. If a state expands its Medicaid program, existing Medicaid limits apply.

SCHIP regulations provide certain protections to enrolled children, including access to health care specialists, access to emergency services when and where the need arises, an assurance that doctors and patients can openly discuss treatment options, and access to a fair, unbiased and timely appeals process.

Initiatives to Prevent Infant Mortality

The Department of Health and Human Services supports a wide range of programs designed to prevent infant mortality. These efforts include programs to improve access to prenatal and newborn care, including Healthy Start, Medicaid and the State Children's Health Insurance Program, discussed above.

The Healthy Start program extends the availability and accessibility of prenatal health care in more than 100 communities nationwide with higher-than-average infant mortality rates. Under the Medicaid program, eligible mothers are provided access to prenatal care and health coverage for millions of infants from low-income families. Families are offered assistance to obtain well-baby screenings that can identify and treat health problems. As set forth above, under SCHIP, children from families who are not eligible for Medicaid but cannot afford private health care coverage, receive comprehensive health care under the government subsidized health care program.

Although maternal and infant health has improved, and the nation's infant mortality rate has fallen from 20 deaths per 1,000 live births in 1970 to 6.9 deaths in 2000, problems persist. For example, the infant mortality rate among African-American children is more than double that for white children. In 1999, the mortality rate for white infants decreased 3 percent to 5.8 deaths per 1,000 live births, while the rate for black infants was 14.6, not statistically different from the 1998 rate.

Early prenatal care has contributed greatly to the reduction of infant mortality. Early and continuous prenatal care helps identify conditions and behavior that can result in low birthweight babies, such as smoking, drug and alcohol abuse, and inadequate weight gain during pregnancy. In 2000, 83.2 percent of mothers began prenatal care within the first trimester of pregnancy. Unfortunately, teenage mothers were the least likely to obtain prenatal care in their first trimester of pregnancy.

Initiatives to Reduce Teen Pregnancy

It is recognized that infants born to teenage mothers are at higher risk of being born low birthweight babies and have a higher mortality rate. The Department of Health and Human Services funds teen pregnancy prevention programs in more than 2,200 communities, focusing on abstinence and personal responsibility.

CHILD CARE

The Personal Responsibility and Work Opportunity Reconciliation Act of 1996

The Personal Responsibility and Work Opportunity Reconciliation Act (PRWORA) overhauled the child care system and consolidated three former child care programs into a single, integrated child care system. Funding under the Act is combined with the discretionary funding of the Child Care and Development Block Grant. This combined funding is referred to as The Child Care and Development Fund (CCDF).

The Act also provided the states with the flexibility to transfer up to 30 percent of their Temporary Assistance to Needy Families (TANF) block grant funding to CCDF, as well as to designate TANF funds directly to child care services to assist in promoting welfare recipients' ability to work and achieve self-sufficiency.

The Child Care and Development Fund

The Child Care and Development Fund (CCDF) assists low income families, families receiving temporary public assistance, and those transitioning from public assistance, in obtaining child care so they can work or attend training and education programs. Subsidized child care services are available to eligible families through certificates or contracts with providers. Under this program, parents may select any legally operating child care provider.

A national directory of ACF Child Care and Development Fund Contacts is set forth at Appendix 11.

Improving Child Care Quality

Under the Act, at least 4 percent of CCDF funds must be used to improve the quality of child care. Child care providers serving children funded by CCDF must meet basic health and safety requirements set by the states. The health and safety requirements address: (i) prevention and control of infectious diseases, including immunizations; (ii) building and physical premises safety; and (iii) minimum health and safety training for child care providers.

School-Age Child Care Initiatives

Thirty-five percent of the children whose care was subsidized through CCDF in 1999 were aged 6 to 12 years. Many states are using quality and subsidy dollars to make additional investments in school-age care. The U.S. Department of Health and Human Services joined with the Department of Education in implementing the 21st Century Learning Centers Program, which includes funds to increase the availability of care for school-age children and youth during non-school hours.

The Head Start Program

Head Start is a national program which was established in 1965 to provide comprehensive developmental services for low-income, pre-school children ages three to five, as well as social services for their families. In 2002, the Head Start program is expected to serve approximately 915,000 children, 225,000 of which receive full-day, full-year services. The remainder attend part-day preschool programs that usually follow a school-year schedule.

The major components of the Head Start program include the following:

1. Education

The Head Start program operates an educational program designed to meet the needs of each child, the community served, and its ethnic and cultural characteristics. Every child receives a variety of learning experiences to foster intellectual, social, and emotional growth.

2. Health Initiative

The Head Start program emphasizes the importance of the early identification of health problems. Every child is involved in a comprehensive health program, which includes immunizations, medical, dental, and mental health, and nutritional services.

3. Parent Involvement

The Head Start program involves parents in parent education, program planning, and operating activities. The program includes classes and workshops on child development for parents.

The Head Start program also identifies specific family needs and provides referrals; family need assessments; recruitment and enrollment of children; emergency assistance and/or crisis intervention, and operates community outreach programs.

The Migrant Head Start Program

The Migrant Head Start program provides the same services as the regular Head Start program, with certain modifications to meet the specific needs of migrant farmworker families. The Migrant Head Start program emphasizes the child care and developmental needs of infants, toddlers and pre-school age children, so that they will not have to be cared for in the fields. Infants as young as 6 weeks of age are served in Migrant

Head Start centers. In order to be eligible for the program, families must meet the annual Head Start poverty income guidelines.

The Early Head Start Program

In 1994, the Head Start Act Amendments established the Early Head Start program, which expands the benefits of early childhood development to low income families with children under three, and to pregnant women. The purpose of the Early Head Start program is to: (i) enhance the younger child's physical, social, emotional and cognitive development; (ii) enable parents to be better caregivers of and teachers to their young children; and (iii) help parents meet their own self-sufficiency goals, including economic independence.

Head Start Initiatives of 2002

In April 2002, President Bush announced an Early Childhood Initiative to improve early education for children that included new steps to further strengthen the Head Start program. The initiatives include a new accountability system to ensure that every Head Start center assesses standards of learning in early literacy, language and numerical skills, and implementation of a national training project in pre-reading and language techniques for the nation's 50,000 Head Start teachers.

A directory of State Collaboration Offices for the Head Start Program is set forth at Appendix 12.

CHILD SUPPORT

The Child Support Enforcement Program, a partnership among federal, state and local agencies, helps families by promoting family self-sufficiency and child well-being. Under this program, state child support agencies locate non-custodial parents, establish paternity if necessary, establish orders for support, and collect child support payments for families. Families seeking government child support services must apply directly through their state agency.

Child support services are available to a parent with custody of a child who has a parent living outside of the home. Services are available automatically for families receiving assistance under the Temporary Assistance for Needy Families (TANF) program and current child support collected reimburses the state and federal governments for TANF payments made to the family. Individuals who are not on public assistance can also apply for child support services and child support payments collected on their behalf are sent directly to the family.

Under the program, states also receive federal grants to help non-custodial parents gain access to, and visitation with, their children. These programs provide mediation, counseling, parenting education, visitation programs, and the development of visitation and custody guidelines. There are also programs in a number of states to promote responsible fatherhood and encourage marriage.

CHAPTER 8:
THE DEPARTMENT OF HEALTH AND HUMAN SERVICES

IN GENERAL

The U.S. Department of Health and Human Services (HHS) is the federal government's principal agency for protecting the health of Americans and providing essential human services, especially for those who are least able to help themselves. HHS works with state and local governments to provide these services.

The U.S. Department of Health and Human Services Information and Hotline Directory is set forth at Appendix 13.

The Department's programs are administered by 11 HHS operating divisions. The primary agency which addresses the needs of the underprivileged population is the Administration for Children and Families (ACF), which is further discussed below. The other HHS operating divisions include the following:

The Administration on Aging

The Administration on Aging (AoA) is the federal agency which represents the interests and concerns of the elderly population. The AoA administers key federal programs mandated under various titles of the Older Americans Act. These programs help vulnerable older persons remain in their own homes by providing supportive services. For example, through the Older Americans Act nutrition programs, AoA provides meals served in senior centers and other group settings; meals delivered to frail, homebound elders, commonly known as "meals on wheels;" transportation; nutrition counseling; health education activities, and related efforts. AoA also funds health promotion and disease prevention efforts by states and local communities, which are targeted to assist the elderly population.

The Agency for Healthcare Research and Quality

The Agency for Healthcare Research and Quality (AHRQ) is the lead agency charged with supporting research designed to improve the quality of health care, reduce its cost, improve patient safety, address medical errors, and broaden access to essential services.

Center for Disease Control and Protection

The Center for Disease Control and Prevention (CDC) provides a system of health surveillance to monitor and prevent disease outbreaks, implement disease prevention strategies, and maintain national health statistics. The CDC also provides for immunization services, workplace safety, and environmental disease prevention.

Centers for Medicare and Medicaid Services

The Centers for Medicare and Medicaid Services (CMS) administer the Medicare and Medicaid programs, which provide health care to about one in every four Americans. Medicare provides health insurance for more than 39 million elderly and disabled Americans. Medicaid, a joint federal-state program, provides health coverage for more than 34 million low-income persons, including nearly 18 million children, and nursing home coverage for low-income elderly. CMS also administers the new Children's Health Insurance Program through approved state plans that cover more than 2.2 million children.

The Food and Drug Administration

The Food and Drug Administration (FDA) assures the safety of foods, cosmetics, pharmaceuticals, biological products and medical devices.

Health Resources and Services Administration

The Health Resources and Services Administration (HRSA) provides access to essential health services for people who are poor, uninsured, or who live in rural and urban neighborhoods where health care is scarce. HRSA also supports programs that ensure healthy mothers and children, increase the number and diversity of health care professionals in underserved communities.

Indian Health Service

The Indian Health Service (IHS) operates 37 hospitals, 60 health centers, 3 school health centers, and 46 health stations. It also assists 34 urban Indian health centers. Services are provided to nearly 1.5 million

American Indians and Alaska Natives of 557 Federally recognized tribes.

National Institutes of Health

The National Institutes of Health (NIH) is the world's foremost medical research organization, encompassing 18 separate health institutes. NIH supports approximately 35,000 research projects nationwide in diseases like cancer, Alzheimer's, diabetes, arthritis, heart ailments and AIDS. NIH also operates the National Center for Complementary and Alternative Medicine and the National Library of Medicine.

The Substance Abuse and Mental Health Services Administration

The Substance Abuse and Mental Health Services Administration (SAMHSA) works to improve the quality and availability of substance abuse prevention, addiction treatment and mental health services, and provides funding to the states to support and maintain substance abuse and mental health services through federal block grants.

THE ADMINISTRATION FOR CHILDREN AND FAMILIES

The Administration for Children and Families (ACF) is responsible for approximately 60 programs that promote the economic and social well-being of families, children, individuals and communities. Programs administered by ACF which are of particular importance to the underprivileged population include: (i) The Temporary Assistance to Needy Families (TANF) program; (ii) The national Child Support Enforcement system; (iii) the Head Start program; and (iv) funding for child care programs aimed at providing assistance to low income families, all of which are further discussed elsewhere in this almanac. ACF also supports state programs to provide for foster care and adoption assistance and prevent child abuse and domestic violence.

A directory of regional offices of the Administration for Children and Families is set forth at Appendix 14.

ACF oversees and funds a broad spectrum of programs, along with state and local agencies. These agencies provide direct services and assistance to those eligible to receive help under ACF legislative authorities. ACF's mission is to promote economic independence for families and individuals through its programs.

ACF Programs

In addition to the ACF programs described above, which are discussed more fully elsewhere in this almanac, ACF also administers the following programs to assist the economically underprivileged population:

The Low Income Home Energy Assistance Program

The Low Income Home Energy Assistance Program (LIHEAP) is a federally funded program that provides grants to states, territories, Native American tribes, and tribal organizations that wish to assist low-income households in meeting the costs of home heating and cooling needs. The amount of each grant to a state is determined by a formula established by Congress.

LIHEAP payments may be made directly to eligible households or to home energy suppliers who comply with the legislative provisions. LIHEAP funds can also be used to help low-income households deal with energy-related crises or pay for repairs to make their homes more energy efficient.

A directory of regional offices of the Low Income Home Energy Assistance Program (LIHEAP) is set forth at Appendix 15.

Programs for Runaways and Homeless Youth

ACF also administers programs to assist homeless youth with making the transition to independent living. The Basic Center Program provides grants to community-based public and private agencies to provide outreach, crisis intervention, temporary shelter, counseling, family reunification and aftercare services to runaway and homeless youth and their families.

The Transitional Living Program helps homeless youth ages 16 through 21 make a successful transition to self-sufficient living. Its goal is to avoid long-term dependency on social services by homeless youths by funding comprehensive services in a supervised living arrangement for up to 18 months.

ACF's Street Outreach Program provides grants to eligible private, non-profit agencies for street-based outreach, education and referral services for runaway, homeless and street youth who have been subjected to, or are at risk of being subjected to sexual abuse.

ASSISTING THE HOMELESS

In General

Each year about 1 percent of the U.S. population—2 to 3 million people—experience homelessness. Homelessness is especially pronounced among those who are poor. Between 5 to 6 percent of the poor population will experience homelessness in any given year. While some individuals may be homeless for only a short period of time, approximately 200,000 individuals are chronically homeless.

The U.S. Department of Health and Human Services works with the Department of Housing and Urban Development (HUD) and other federal, state and local agencies to improve the services provided to homeless individuals.

Individuals who are homeless may be eligible to receive assistance from a number of the department's mainstream programs including Medicare, Medicaid, Temporary Assistance for Needy Families (TANF) and programs providing health care, mental health, social and substance abuse services.

Demographics

According to the federal Interagency Council on the Homeless, more than two-thirds of people who are homeless and receiving services are male and more than half are nonwhite. Almost 40 percent have less than a high school diploma. Almost half of the homeless population have never been married, and 60 percent of homeless women and 41 percent of homeless men have minor children. Over a quarter of these children live with their homeless parent.

Two-thirds of those surveyed reported mental illness, substance abuse disorder or both during the previous month. In the area of physical health, 26 percent reported a current acute infectious condition and 46 percent identified a chronic condition such as diabetes or hypertension.

HHS Homeless Programs

HHS agencies support a number of programs that are aimed at assisting homeless people in obtaining and maintaining stable housing and addressing many of the other needs specifically involving the homeless population. The HRSA Health Care for the Homeless Program is designed to improves access to primary health care and mental health and substance abuse services by homeless individuals.

SAMHSA administers programs for people who are homeless and living with serious mental illnesses, substance abuse or both. The Projects for

Assistance in Transition from Homelessness (PATH) program supports community-based services for people with serious mental illnesses and substance use disorders, who are either homeless or at risk of homelessness.

In addition to the programs and services focused specifically on home-lessness, mainstream HHS programs that serve millions of low-income Americans and people with disabilities, such as Medicare, Medicaid, and TANF, also provide eligible homeless individuals with services and support.

APPENDIX 1:
DIRECTORY OF STATE HUMAN SERVICES ADMINISTRATORS

STATE	AGENCY	ADDRESS	TELEPHONE	FAX
ALABAMA	Department of Human Resources	50 Ripley Street, Montgomery, AL 36130-4000	(334) 242-1160	(334) 242-0198
ALASKA	Department of Health and Social Services	PO Box 110601, Juneau, AK 99811-0601	(907) 465-3030	(907) 465-3068
ARIZONA	Department of Economic Security	P.O. Box 6123, Site Code 010A, Phoenix, AZ 85005	(602) 542-5678	(602) 542-5339
ARKANSAS	Department of Human Services	329 Donaghey Plaza South, PO Box 1437, Little Rock, AR 72203-1437	(501) 682-8650	(501) 682-6836
CALIFORNIA	Health and Human Services Agency	1600 Ninth Street, Room 460, Sacramento, CA 95814	(916) 654-3345	(916) 654-3343
COLORADO	Department of Human Services	1575 Sherman Street, 8th Floor, Denver, CO 80203-1714	(303) 866-5096	(303) 866-4740
CONNECTICUT	Department of Social Services	25 Sigourney Street, Hartford, CT 06106-2055	(860) 424-5008	(860) 424-5129

STATE	AGENCY	ADDRESS	TELEPHONE	FAX
DELAWARE	Health and Social Services	Herman M. Holloway Sr. Campus, Main Administration Building, 1st Floor, 1901 N. DuPont Highway, New Castle, DE 19720	(302) 577-4502	(302) 577-4510
DISTRICT OF COLUMBIA	Department of Human Services	801 East Building, 2700 Martin Luther King Jr. Ave. SE, Washington, DC 200320247	(202) 279-6016	(202) 279-6014
FLORIDA	Department of Children and Families	Building 1, Room 202, 1317 Winewood Boulevard, Tallahassee, FL 32399-0700	(850) 487-1111	(850) 922-2993
GEORGIA	Department of Human Resources, Division of Family & Children Services	2 Peachtree Street, Atlanta, GA 30303	(404) 657-766	(404) 657-5105
HAWAII	Department of Human Services,	PO Box 339, 1390 Miller Street, Room 209, Honolulu, HI 96813	(808) 586-4997	(808) 586-4890
IDAHO	Department of Health & Welfare	P.O. Box 83720, 450 West State Street, 10th Floor, Boise, ID 83720-0036	(208) 334-5500	(208) 334-6558

STATE	AGENCY	ADDRESS	TELEPHONE	FAX
ILLINOIS	Department of Human Services	Harris Building, 3rd Floor, 210 South Grand Avenue East, Springfield, IL 62762	(217) 557-1601	(217) 557-1647
INDIANA	Family and Social Services Administration	402 West Washington Street, Room W-461, Indianapolis, IN 46204	(317) 233-4690	(317) 233-4693
IOWA	Department of Human Services	East 13th Street and Walnut, Hoover State Office Building, Des Moines, IA 50319-0114	(515) 281-5452	(515) 281-4597
KANSAS	Department of Social and Rehabilitation Services	Docking State Office Building, 6th Floor, 915 SW Harrison, Topeka, KS 66612-1570	(913) 296-3271	(913) 296-4685
KENTUCKY	Cabinet for Families & Children	275 East Main Street, 4th Floor, Frankfort, KY 40621	(502) 564-7130	(502) 564-3866
LOUISIANA	Department of Social Services	P.O. Box 3776, 755 N. 3rd Street, Room 201, Baton Rouge, LA 70821	(225) 342-0286	(225) 342-8636
MAINE	Department of Human Services	11 State House Station, 221 State Street, Augusta, ME 04333	(207) 287-2736	(207) 287-3005

STATE	AGENCY	ADDRESS	TELEPHONE	FAX
MARYLAND	Department of Human Resources, Saratoga State Center	311 West Saratoga Street, 10th Floor, Baltimore, MD 21201	(410) 767-7109	(410) 333-0099
MASSACHUSETTS	Department of Transitional Assistance	600 Washington Street, Boston, MA 02111	(617) 348-8410	(617) 348-8575
MICHIGAN	Family Independence Agency	235 South Grand Avenue, Lansing, MI 48909	(517) 373-2000	(517) 335-6101
MINNESOTA	Department of Human Services	444 Lafayette Road, St. Paul, MN 55155-3815	(651) 296-2701	(651) 296-5868
MISSISSIPPI	Department of Human Services	750 North State Street, Jackson, MS 39202	(601) 359-4480	(601) 359-4477
MISSOURI	Department of Social Services	Broadway State Office Building, 221 W. High Street, Jefferson City, MO 65102	(573) 751-4815	(573) 751-3203
MONTANA	Department of Public Health and Human Services	111 North Sanders, P.O. Box 4210, Helena, MT 59604-4210	(406) 444-5622	(406) 444-1970
NEBRASKA	Department of Health and Human Services	P.O. Box 59604, Lincoln, NE 68509-5044	(402) 471-9106	(402) 471-0820
NEVADA	Department of Human Resources	505 East King Street, Suite 600, Carson City, NV 89710	(775) 687-4730	(775) 687-4733

STATE	AGENCY	ADDRESS	TELEPHONE	FAX
NEW HAMPSHIRE	Department of Health and Human Services	State Office Park South, 129 Pleasant St., Brown Bldg., Concord, NH 03301-3857	(603) 271-4331	(603) 271-4232
NEW JERSEY	Department of Human Services	P.O. Box 700, Trenton, NJ 08625-0700	(609) 292-3717	(609) 292-3824
NEW MEXICO	Human Services Department	P.O. Box 2348, 2009 South Pacheco, Santa Fe, NM 87504-2348	(505) 827-7750	(505) 827-6286
NEW YORK	Office of Children and Family Services	52 Washington Street, Rensselaer, NY 12144	(518) 473-8437	(518) 473-9131
NORTH CAROLINA	Department of Health and Human Services	101 Blair Drive, Raleigh, NC 27603	(919) 733-4534	(919) 715-4645
NORTH DAKOTA	Department of Human Services	State Capitol - Judicial Wing, 600 East Boulevard, Bismarck, ND 58505	(701) 328-2310	(701) 328-1545
OHIO	Department of Jobs and Family Services	30 East Broad Street, 32nd Floor, Columbus, OH 43266-0423	(614) 466-6282	(614) 466-2815
OKLAHOMA	Department of Human Services	P.O. Box 25352, Oklahoma City, OK 73125-0352	(405) 521-3646	(405) 521-6458
OREGON	Department of Human Services	500 Summer Street N.E., Salem, OR 97310-1012	(503) 945-5944	(503) 378-2897

STATE	AGENCY	ADDRESS	TELEPHONE	FAX
PENNSYLVANIA	Department of Public Welfare	P.O. Box 2675, Harrisburg, PA 17105-2675	(717) 787-2600	(717) 772-2062
RHODE ISLAND	Rhode Island Department of Human Services	600 New London Avenue, Cranston, RI 02920	(401) 462-2121	(401) 462-3677
SOUTH CAROLINA	Department of Social Services	1535 Confederate Avenue, P.O. Box 1520, Columbia, SC 29202-1520	(803) 898-7360	(803) 898-7276
SOUTH DAKOTA	Department of Human Services	700 Governors Drive, Pierre, SD 57501-2291	(605) 773-3165	(605) 773-4855
TENNESSEE	Department of Human Services	400 Deaderick Street, Nashville, TN 37248-0200	(615) 313-4700	(615) 741-4165
TEXAS	Department of Human Services	701 West 51st Street, P.O. Box 149030, Mail Code W-619, Austin, TX 78714-9030	(512) 438-3030	(512) 438-4220
UTAH	Department of Human Services	120 North 200 West, Room 319, Salt Lake City, UT 84145-0500	(801) 538-3998	(801) 538-4016
VERMONT	Department of Social Welfare	103 South Main Street, Waterbury, VT 05671-1201	(802) 241-2853	(802) 241-2830
VIRGINIA	Health & Human Resources	202 North 9th Street, Suite 622, Richmond, VA 23219	(804) 786-7765	(804) 371-6984

STATE	AGENCY	ADDRESS	TELEPHONE	FAX
WASHINGTON	Department of Social and Health Services	115 Washington Street SE, P.O. Box 45010, Olympia, WA 98504-5010	(360) 902-7800	(360) 902-7848
WEST VIRGINIA	Department of Health and Human Resources	350 Capitol Street, Room 730, Charleston, WV 25301-3711	(304) 558-0999	(304) 558-4194
WISCONSIN	Department of Health and Family Services	P.O. Box 7850, Madison, WI 53707-7850	(608) 266-9622	(608) 266-7882
WYOMING	Department of Family Services	Hathaway Building, 2300 Capitol Avenue, Cheyenne, WY 82002-0490	(307) 777-7564	(307) 777-7747

APPENDIX 2:
U.S. DEPARTMENT OF HEALTH AND HUMAN SERVICES POVERTY GUIDELINES (2002)

FAMILY SIZE	CONTINENTAL U.S.	ALASKA	HAWAII
1	$ 8,860	$11,080	$10,200
2	11,940	14,930	13,740
3	15,020	18,780	17,280
4	18,100	22,630	20,820
5	21,180	26,480	24,360
6	24,260	30,330	27,900
7	27,340	34,180	31,440
8	30,420	38,030	34,980
For Each Additional Person Add:	3,080	3,850	3,540

APPENDIX 3:
PERSONAL RESPONSIBILITY AND WORK OPPORTUNITY RECONCILIATION ACT (H.R. 3734)—TABLE OF CONTENTS AND FINDINGS

SECTION 1. SHORT TITLE.

This Act may be cited as the "Personal Responsibility and Work Opportunity Reconciliation Act of 1996".

SEC. 2. TABLE OF CONTENTS. [OMITTED]

The Table of Contents for this Act is as follows:

Subtitle C—Attribution of Income and Affidavits of Support

Sec. 421. Federal attribution of sponsor's income and resources to alien.

Sec. 422. Authority for States to provide for attribution of sponsors income and resources to the alien with respect to State programs.

Sec. 423. Requirements for sponsor's affidavit of support.

Subtitle D—General Provisions

Sec. 431. Definitions.

Sec. 432. Verification of eligibility for Federal public benefits.

Sec. 433. Statutory construction.

Sec. 434. Communication between State and local government agencies and the Immigration and Naturalization Service.

Sec. 435. Qualifying quarters.

Subtitle E—Conforming Amendments Relating to Assisted Housing

Sec. 441. Conforming amendments relating to assisted housing.

Subtitle F—Earning Income Credit Denied to Unauthorized Employees

Sec. 451. Earned income credit denied to individuals not authorized to be employed in the United States.

TITLE V—CHILD PROTECTION

Sec. 501. Authority of States to make foster care maintenance payments on behalf of children in any private child care institution.

Sec. 502. Extension of enhanced match for implementation of statewide automated child welfare information systems.

Sec. 503. National random sample study of child welfare.

Sec. 504. Redesignation of section 1123.

Sec. 505. Kinship care.

TITLE VI—CHILD CARE

Sec. 601. Short title and references.

Sec. 602. Goals.

TITLE VII—CHILD NUTRITION PROGRAMS

Subtitle A—National School Lunch Act

Subtitle B—Child Nutrition Act of 1966

Subtitle C—Miscellaneous Provisions

TITLE VIII—FOOD STAMPS AND COMMODITY DISTRIBUTION

Subtitle A—Food Stamp Program

Subtitle C—Electronic Benefit Transfer Systems

Sec. 891. Provisions to encourage electronic benefit transfer systems.

TITLE IX—MISCELLANEOUS

Sec. 901. Appropriation by State legislatures.

Sec. 902. Sanctioning for testing positive for controlled substances.

Sec. 903. Elimination of housing assistance with respect to fugitive felons and probation and parole violators.

Sec. 904. Sense of the Senate regarding the inability of the noncustodial parent to pay child support.

Sec. 905. Establishing national goals to prevent teenage pregnancies.

Sec. 906. Sense of the Senate regarding enforcement of statutory rape laws.

Sec. 907. Provisions to encourage electronic benefit transfer systems.

Sec. 908. Reduction of block grants to States for social services; use of vouchers.

Sec. 909. Rules relating to denial of earned income credit on basis of disqualified income.

Sec. 910. Modification of adjusted gross income definition for earned income credit.

Sec. 911. Fraud under means-tested welfare and public assistance programs.

Sec. 912. Abstinence education.

Sec. 913. Change in reference.

TITLE I—BLOCK GRANTS FOR TEMPORARY ASSISTANCE FOR NEEDY FAMILIES

SEC. 101. FINDINGS.

The Congress makes the following findings:

(1) Marriage is the foundation of a successful society.

(2) Marriage is an essential institution of a successful society which promotes the interests of children.

(3) Promotion of responsible fatherhood and motherhood is integral to successful child rearing and the well-being of children.

(4) In 1992, only 54 percent of single-parent families with children had a child support order established and, of that 54 percent, only about one-half received the full amount due. Of the cases enforced through the public child support enforcement system, only 18 percent of the caseload has a collection.

(5) The number of individuals receiving aid to families with dependent children (in this section referred to as "AFDC") has more than tripled since 1965. More than two-thirds of these recipients are children. Eighty-nine percent of children receiving AFDC benefits now live in homes in which no father is present.

(A)(i) The average monthly number of children receiving AFDC benefits— (I) was 3,300,000 in 1965; (II) was 6,200,000 in 1970; (III) was 7,400,000 in 1980; and (IV) was 9,300,000 in 1992. (ii) While the number of children receiving AFDC benefits increased nearly threefold between 1965 and 1992, the total number of children in the United States aged 0 to 18 has declined by 5.5 percent.

(B) The Department of Health and Human Services has estimated that 12,000,000 children will receive AFDC benefits within 10 years.

(C) The increase in the number of children receiving public assistance is closely related to the increase in births to unmarried women. Between 1970 and 1991, the percentage of live births to unmarried women increased nearly threefold, from 10.7 percent to 29.5 percent.

(6) The increase of out-of-wedlock pregnancies and births is well documented as follows:

(A) It is estimated that the rate of nonmarital teen pregnancy rose 23 percent from 54 pregnancies per 1,000 unmarried teenagers in 1976 to 66.7 pregnancies in 1991. The overall rate of nonmarital pregnancy rose 14 percent from 90.8 pregnancies per 1,000 unmarried women in 1980 to 103 in both 1991 and 1992. In contrast, the overall pregnancy rate for married couples decreased 7.3 percent between 1980 and 1991, from 126.9 pregnancies per 1,000 married women in 1980 to 117.6 pregnancies in 1991.

(B) The total of all out-of-wedlock births between 1970 and 1991 has risen from 10.7 percent to 29.5 percent and if the current trend continues, 50 percent of all births by the year 2015 will be out-of-wedlock.

(7) An effective strategy to combat teenage pregnancy must address the issue of male responsibility, including statutory rape culpability and prevention. The increase of teenage pregnancies among the youngest girls is particularly severe and is linked to predatory sexual practices by men who are significantly older.

(A) It is estimated that in the late 1980's, the rate for girls age 14 and under giving birth increased 26 percent.

(B) Data indicates that at least half of the children born to teenage mothers are fathered by adult men. Available data suggests that almost 70 percent of births to teenage girls are fathered by men over age 20.

(C) Surveys of teen mothers have revealed that a majority of such mothers have histories of sexual and physical abuse, primarily with older adult men.

(8) The negative consequences of an out-of-wedlock birth on the mother, the child, the family, and society are well documented as follows:

(A) Young women 17 and under who give birth outside of marriage are more likely to go on public assistance and to spend more years on welfare once enrolled. These combined effects of "younger and longer" increase total AFDC costs per household by 25 percent to 30 percent for 17-year-olds.

(B) Children born out-of-wedlock have a substantially higher risk of being born at a very low or moderately low birth weight.

(C) Children born out-of-wedlock are more likely to experience low verbal cognitive attainment, as well as more child abuse, and neglect.

(D) Children born out-of-wedlock were more likely to have lower cognitive scores, lower educational aspirations, and a greater likelihood of becoming teenage parents themselves.

(E) Being born out-of-wedlock significantly reduces the chances of the child growing up to have an intact marriage.

(F) Children born out-of-wedlock are 3 times more likely to be on welfare when they grow up.

(9) Currently 35 percent of children in single-parent homes were born out-of-wedlock, nearly the same percentage as that of children

in single-parent homes whose parents are divorced (37 percent). While many parents find themselves, through divorce or tragic circumstances beyond their control, facing the difficult task of raising children alone, nevertheless, the negative consequences of raising children in single-parent homes are well documented as follows:

(A) Only 9 percent of married-couple families with children under 18 years of age have income below the national poverty level. In contrast, 46 percent of female-headed households with children under 18 years of age are below the national poverty level.

(B) Among single-parent families, nearly 1 out of 2 of the mothers who never married received AFDC while only 1 out of 5 of divorced mothers received AFDC.

(C) Children born into families receiving welfare assistance are 3 times more likely to be on welfare when they reach adulthood than children not born into families receiving welfare.

(D) Mothers under 20 years of age are at the greatest risk of bearing low birth weight babies.

(E) The younger the single-parent mother, the less likely she is to finish high school.

(F) Young women who have children before finishing high school are more likely to receive welfare assistance for a longer period of time.

(G) Between 1985 and 1990, the public cost of births to teenage mothers under the aid to families with dependent children program, the food stamp program, and the medicaid program has been estimated at $120,000,000,000.

(H) The absence of a father in the life of a child has a negative effect on school performance and peer adjustment.

(I) Children of teenage single parents have lower cognitive scores, lower educational aspirations, and a greater likelihood of becoming teenage parents themselves.

(J) Children of single-parent homes are 3 times more likely to fail and repeat a year in grade school than are children from intact 2-parent families.

(K) Children from single-parent homes are almost 4 times more likely to be expelled or suspended from school.

(L) Neighborhoods with larger percentages of youth aged 12 through 20 and areas with higher percentages of single-parent households have higher rates of violent crime.

(M) Of those youth held for criminal offenses within the State juvenile justice system, only 29.8 percent lived primarily in a home with both parents. In contrast to these incarcerated youth, 73.9 percent of the 62,800,000 children in the Nation's resident population were living with both parents.

(10) Therefore, in light of this demonstration of the crisis in our Nation, it is the sense of the Congress that prevention of out-of-wedlock pregnancy and reduction in out-of-wedlock birth are very important Government interests and the policy contained in part A of title IV of the Social Security Act (as amended by section 103(a) of this Act) is intended to address the crisis.

APPENDIX 4:
U.S. DEPARTMENT OF LABOR—WELFARE TO WORK PROGRAM—REGIONAL OFFICES

STATE	ADDRESS
ALABAMA	Workforce Development Division, 401 Adams Avenue, P.O. Box 5690, Montgomery, Alabama 36103
ALASKA	Employment and Security Division, P.O. Box 25509, Juneau, Alaska 99802
ARKANSAS	Arkansas Employment Security Department, P.O. Box 2981, Little Rock, Arkansas 72202
CALIFORNIA	Job Training Partnership Division, 800 Capitol Mall, MIC 69, Sacramento, California 95814
COLORADO	Colorado Labor Department, Tower 2—Suite 400, 1515 Arapahoe Street, Denver, Colorado 80202
CONNECTICUT	Connecticut Labor Department, 200 Folly Brook Boulevard, Wethersfield, Connecticut 06109
DISTRICT OF COLUMBIA	Office of Workforce Development, Department of Employment Services, 500 C Street, N.W., Suite 301, Washington, D.C. 20001
FLORIDA	Division of Jobs and Benefits, Room 300, Atkins Building, 1320 Executive Center Drive, Tallahassee, Florida 32399
GEORGIA	Georgia Department of Labor, 148 International Boulevard N.E., Suite 650, Atlanta, Georgia 30303
HAWAII	Workforce Development Division, 830 Punchbowl Street, Suite 329, Honolulu, Hawaii 96813
ILLINOIS	Job Training Division, 620 East Adams Street, Springfield, Illinois 62701
INDIANA	Indiana Department of Workforce Development, Indiana Government Center South, SE302, 10 North Senate Avenue, Indianapolis, Indiana 46204

STATE	ADDRESS
IOWA	Iowa Workforce Development, 1000 East Grand Avenue, Des Moines, Iowa 50319
KANSAS,	Kansas Department of Human Resources, Division of Employment and Training, 401 S.W. Topeka Boulevard, Topeka, Kansas 66603
KENTUCKY	Department of Social Insurance, 275 East Main Street, 3C-B, Frankfort, Kentucky 40621
LOUISIANA	Office of Workforce Development, Louisiana Department of Labor, P.O. Box 94094, Baton Rouge, Louisiana 70804
MAINE	Bureau of Employment Services, 55 State House Station, Augusta, Maine 04333
MARYLAND	Department of Labor, Licensing, and Regulations, 500 North Calvert Street, Baltimore, Maryland 21202
MASSACHUSETTS	Department of Labor Workforce Development, One Ashburton Place, 14th Floor, Boston, Massachusetts 02108
MICHIGAN	Michigan Department of Career Development, Office of Workforce Development, 201 North Washington Square, 5th Floor, Lansing, Michigan 48913
MINNESOTA	Minnesota Department of Economic Security, 390 North Robert Street, St. Paul, Minnesota 55101
MISSOURI	Department of Economic Development, Division of Job Development and Training, 2023 St. Mary's Boulevard, Jefferson City, Missouri 65109
MONTANA	Montana Department of Labor and Industry, Office of Program Management, P.O. Box 1728, Helena, Montana 59624
NEBRASKA	Nebraska Department of Labor, 550 South 16th Street, P.O. Box 94600, Lincoln, Nebraska 68509
NEVADA	Nevada State Welfare Division, 2527 North Carson Street, Carson City, Nevada 89706
NEW HAMPSHIRE	New Hampshire Department of Labor, 64 Old Suncook Road, Concord, New Hampshire 03301
NEW JERSEY	New Jersey Department of Labor, Division of Employment and Training, John Fitch Plaza, Trenton, New Jersey 08625

STATE	ADDRESS
NEW MEXICO	New Mexico Department of Labor, 596 Pacheco Street, Santa Fe, New Mexico 87502
NEW YORK	New York State Department of Labor, State Office Building Campus, Room 288, Albany, New York 12240
NORTH CAROLINA	North Carolina Department of Commerce, Division of Workforce Development, 441 North Harrington Street, Raleigh, North Carolina 27603
NORTH DAKOTA	North Dakota Department of Job Services, 1000 East Divide Avenue, P.O. Box 5507, Bismarck, North Dakota 58506
OKLAHOMA	Oklahoma Department of Labor, 2401 North Lincoln, Oklahoma City, Oklahoma 73152
OREGON	Job Workforce, 500 Summer Street NE, Salem, Oregon 97310
PENNSYLVANIA	Bureau of Employment and Training Programs, P.O. Box 2675, Harrisburg, Pennsylvania 17105
RHODE ISLAND	Job Training Partnership Office, 610 Manton Avenue, Providence, Rhode Island 02909
SOUTH CAROLINA	South Carolina Department of Labor, Division of Employment and Training, 1550 Gadsden Street, P.O. Box 1406, Columbia, South Carolina 29202
TENNESSEE	Families First Program and Food Stamps, 400 Deaderick Street, Nashville, Tennessee 37215
TEXAS	Texas Workforce Commission, Workforce Development, 101 East 15th Street, Rom 504BT, Austin, Texas 78778
VERMONT	Vermont Department of Employment and Training, 5 Green Mountain Drive, P.O. Box 488, Montpelier, Vermont 05601
VIRGINIA	Virginia Department of Social Services, 730 East Broad Street, Richmond, Virginia 23219
WASHINGTON	Employment Security Department, Training and Employment, P.O. Box 9046, Olympia, Washington 98507
WEST VIRGINIA	Employment Services Division, 112 California Avenue, Charleston, West Virginia 25305

STATE	ADDRESS
WISCONSIN	Division of Workforce Excellence, P.O. Box 7972, 201 East Washington Avenue, Room 201X, Madison, Wisconsin 53707

APPENDIX 5:
TEMPORARY ASSISTANCE TO NEEDY FAMILIES (TANF) WORK PARTICIPATION RATES

FISCAL YEAR	ALL FAMILIES		TWO-PARENT FAMILIES	
	PARTICIPATION RATE	WEEKLY HOURS OF WORK	PARTICIPATION RATE	WEEKLY HOURS OF WORK
1997	25%	20	75%	35
1998	30%	20	75%	35
1999	35%	25	90%	35
2000	40%	30	90%	35
2001	45%	30	90%	35
2002	50%	30	90%	35

APPENDIX 6:
SELECTED PROVISIONS OF THE FEDERAL FOOD STAMP ACT—TITLE 7—CH. 51

SEC. 2011.—CONGRESSIONAL DECLARATION OF POLICY

It is declared to be the policy of Congress, in order to promote the general welfare, to safeguard the health and well-being of the Nation's population by raising levels of nutrition among low-income households. Congress finds that the limited food purchasing power of low-income households contributes to hunger and malnutrition among members of such households. Congress further finds that increased utilization of food in establishing and maintaining adequate national levels of nutrition will promote the distribution in a beneficial manner of the Nation's agricultural abundance and will strengthen the Nation's agricultural economy, as well as result in more orderly marketing and distribution of foods. To alleviate such hunger and malnutrition, a food stamp program is herein authorized which will permit low-income households to obtain a more nutritious diet through normal channels of trade by increasing food purchasing power for all eligible households who apply for participation.

SEC. 2012.—DEFINITIONS [OMITTED]

SEC. 2012A.—PUBLICLY OPERATED COMMUNITY HEALTH CENTERS [OMITTED]

SEC. 2013.—ESTABLISHMENT OF PROGRAM

(a) Use of coupons; redeemability

Subject to the availability of funds appropriated under section 2027 of this title, the Secretary is authorized to formulate and administer a food stamp program under which, at the request of the State agency, eligible households within the State shall be provided an opportunity to obtain a more nutritious diet through the issuance to them of an allotment, except that a State may not participate in the food stamp program if the Secretary determines that State or local sales taxes are collected within that State on purchases of food made with coupons issued under this chapter. The coupons so received by such households shall be used only to purchase food from retail food stores which have been approved for participation in the food stamp program. Coupons issued and used as provided in this chapter shall be redeemable at face value by the Secretary through the facilities of the Treasury of the United States.

(b) Distribution of federally donated foods [Omitted]

(c) Regulations; transmittal of copy of regulations to Congressional committees prior to issuance [Omitted]

House of Representatives and the Committee on Agriculture, Nutrition, and Forestry of the Senate a copy of the regulation with a detailed statement justifying iT.

SEC. 2014.—ELIGIBLE HOUSEHOLDS

(a) Income and other financial resources as substantial limiting factors in obtaining more nutritious diet; recipients under Social Security Act

Participation in the food stamp program shall be limited to those households whose incomes and other financial resources, held singly or in joint ownership, are determined to be a substantial limiting factor in permitting them to obtain a more nutritious diet. Notwithstanding any other provisions of this chapter except sections 2015(b), 2015(d)(2), and 2015(g) of this title and the third sentence of section 2012(i) of this title, households in which each member receives benefits under a State program funded under part A of title IV of the Social Security Act (42 U.S.C. 601 et seq.), supplemental security income benefits under title XVI of the Social Security Act (42 U.S.C. 1381 et seq.), or aid to the aged, blind, or disabled under title I, X, XIV, or XVI of the Social Security Act (42 U.S.C. 301 et seq., 1201 et seq., 1351 et seq., or 1381 et seq.), shall be eligible to participate in the food stamp program. Except for sections 2015, 2025(e)(1), and the third sentence of section 2012(i) of this title, households in which each member receives benefits under a State or local general assistance program that complies with standards established by the Secretary for ensuring that the program is based on income criteria comparable to or more restrictive than those under subsection (c)(2) of this section, and not limited to one-time emergency payments that cannot be provided for more than one consecutive month, shall be eligible to participate in the food stamp program. Assistance under this program shall be furnished to all eligible households who make application for such participation.

(b) Eligibility standards

Except as otherwise provided in this chapter, the Secretary shall establish uniform national standards of eligibility (other than the income standards for Alaska, Hawaii, Guam, and the Virgin Islands of the United States established in accordance with subsections (c) and (e) of this section) for participation by households in the food stamp program in accordance with the provisions of this section. No plan of operation submitted by a State agency shall be approved unless the standards of eligibility meet those established by the Secretary, and no State agency shall impose any other standards of eligibility as a condition for participating in the program.

(c) Gross income standard

The income standards of eligibility shall be adjusted each October 1 and shall provide that a household shall be ineligible to participate in the food stamp program if—

(1) the household's income (after the exclusions and deductions provided for in subsections (d) and (e) of this section) exceeds the poverty line, as defined in section 673(2) of the Community Services Block Grant Act (42 U.S.C. 9902(2)), for the forty-eight contiguous States and the District of Columbia, Alaska, Hawaii, the Virgin Islands of the United States, and Guam, respectively; and

(2) in the case of a household that does not include an elderly or disabled member, the household's income (after the exclusions provided for in subsection (d) of this section but before the deductions provided for in subsection (e) of this section) exceeds such poverty line by more than 30 per centum. In no event shall the standards of eligibility for the Virgin Islands of the United States or Guam exceed those in the forty-eight contiguous States.

(d) Income excluded in computing household income

Household income for purposes of the food stamp program shall include all income from whatever source excluding only

(1) any gain or benefit which is not in the form of money payable directly to a household (notwithstanding its conversion in whole or in part to direct payments to households pursuant to any demonstration project carried out or authorized under Federal law including

demonstration projects created by the waiver of provisions of Federal law),

(2) any income in the certification period which is received too infrequently or irregularly to be reasonably anticipated, but not in excess of $30 in a quarter, subject to modification by the Secretary in light of subsection (f) of this section,

(3) all educational loans on which payment is deferred, grants, scholarships, fellowships, veterans' educational benefits, and the like (A) awarded to a household member enrolled at a recognized institution of post-secondary education, at a school for the handicapped, in a vocational education program, or in a program that provides for completion of a secondary school diploma or obtaining the equivalent thereof, (B) to the extent that they do not exceed the amount used for or made available as an allowance determined by such school, institution, program, or other grantor, for tuition and mandatory fees (including the rental or purchase of any equipment, materials, and supplies related to the pursuit of the course of study involved), books, supplies, transportation, and other miscellaneous personal expenses (other than living expenses), of the student incidental to attending such school, institution, or program, and (C) to the extent loans include any origination fees and insurance premiums,

(4) all loans other than educational loans on which repayment is deferred,

(5) reimbursements which do not exceed expenses actually incurred and which do not represent a gain or benefit to the household and any allowance a State agency provides no more frequently than annually to families with children on the occasion of those children's entering or returning to school or child care for the purpose of obtaining school clothes (except that no such allowance shall be excluded if the State agency reduces monthly assistance under a State program funded under part A of title IV of the Social Security Act (42 U.S.C. 601 et seq.) in the month for which the allowance is provided): Provided, That no portion of benefits provided under title IV-A of the Social Security Act (42 U.S.C. 601 et seq.), to the extent it is attributable to an adjustment for work-related or child care expenses (except for payments or reimbursements for such expenses made under an employment, education, or training program initiated under such title after September 19, 1988), and no portion of any educational loan on which payment is deferred, grant, scholarship, fellowship, veterans' benefits, and the like that are provided for living expenses, shall be considered such reimbursement,

(6) moneys received and used for the care and maintenance of a third-party beneficiary who is not a household member,

(7) income earned by a child who is a member of the household, who is an elementary or secondary school student, and who is 17 years of age or younger,

(8) moneys received in the form of nonrecurring lump-sum payments, including, but not limited to, income tax refunds, rebates, or credits, cash donations based on need that are received from one or more private nonprofit charitable organizations, but not in excess of $300 in the aggregate in a quarter, retroactive lump-sum social security or railroad retirement pension payments and retroactive lump-sum insurance settlements: Provided, That such payments shall be counted as resources, unless specifically excluded by other laws,

(9) the cost of producing self-employed income, but household income that otherwise is included under this subsection shall be reduced by the extent that the cost of producing self-employment income exceeds the income derived from self-employment as a farmer,

(10) any income that any other Federal law specifically excludes from consideration as income for purposes of determining eligibility for the food stamp program except as otherwise provided in subsection (k) of this section,

(11) (A) any payments or allowances made for the purpose of providing energy assistance under any Federal law (other than part A of title IV of the Social Security Act (42 U.S.C. 601 et seq.)), or (B) a 1-time payment or allowance made under a Federal or State law for the costs of weatherization or emergency repair or replacement of an unsafe or inoperative furnace or other heating or cooling device,

(12) through September 30 of any fiscal year, any increase in income attributable to a cost-of-living adjustment made on or after July 1 of such fiscal year under title II or XVI of the Social Security Act (42 U.S.C. 401 et seq., 1381 et seq.), section 3(a)(1) of the Railroad Retirement Act of 1974 (45 U.S.C. 231b(a)(1)), or section 5312 of title 38, if the household was certified as eligible to participate in the food stamp program or received an allotment in the month immediately preceding the first month in which the adjustment was effective,

(13) any payment made to the household under section 3507 of title 26 (relating to advance payment of earned income credit),

(14) any payment made to the household under section 2015(d)(4)(I) of this title for work related expenses or for dependent care, and

(15) any amounts necessary for the fulfillment of a plan for achieving self-support of a household member as provided under subparagraph (A)(iii) or (B)(iv) of section 1612(b)(4) of the Social Security Act (42 U.S.C. 1382a(b)(4)).

(e) Deductions from income

(1) Standard deduction

The Secretary shall allow a standard deduction for each household in the 48 contiguous States and the District of Columbia, Alaska, Hawaii, Guam, and the Virgin Islands of the United States of $134, $229, $189, $269, and $118, respectively.

(2) Earned income deduction

(A) "Earned income" defined

In this paragraph, the term "earned income" does not include—

(i) income excluded by subsection (d) of this section; or

(ii) any portion of income earned under a work supplementation or support program, as defined under section 2025(b) of this title, that is attributable to public assistance.

(B) Deduction

Except as provided in subparagraph (C), a household with earned income shall be allowed a deduction of 20 percent of all earned income to compensate for taxes, other mandatory deductions from salary, and work expenses.

(C) Exception

The deduction described in subparagraph (B) shall not be allowed with respect to determining an overissuance due to the failure of a household to report earned income in a timely manner.

(3) Dependent care deduction

(A) In general

A household shall be entitled, with respect to expenses (other than excluded expenses described in subparagraph (B)) for dependent care, to a dependent care deduction, the maximum allowable level of which shall be $200 per month for each dependent child under 2 years of age and $175 per month for each other dependent, for the actual cost of payments necessary for the care of a dependent if the care enables a household member to accept or continue employment, or training or education that is preparatory for employment.

(B) Excluded expenses

The excluded expenses referred to in subparagraph (A) are—

(i) expenses paid on behalf of the household by a third party;

(ii) amounts made available and excluded, for the expenses referred to in subparagraph (A), under subsection (d)(3) of this section; and

(iii) expenses that are paid under section 2015(d)(4) of this title.

(4) Deduction for child support payments

(A) In general

A household shall be entitled to a deduction for child support payments made by a household member to or for an individual who is not a member of the household if the household member is legally obligated to make the payments.

(B) Methods for determining amount

The Secretary may prescribe by regulation the methods, including calculation on a retrospective basis, that a State agency shall use to determine the amount of the deduction for child support payments.

(5) Homeless shelter allowance

Under rules prescribed by the Secretary, a State agency may develop a standard homeless shelter allowance, which shall not exceed $143 per month, for such expenses as may reasonably be expected to be incurred by households in which all members are homeless individuals but are not receiving free shelter throughout the month. A State agency that develops the allowance may use the allowance in determining eligibility and allotments for the households. The State agency may make a household with extremely low shelter costs ineligible for the allowance.

(6) Excess medical expense deduction

(A) In general

A household containing an elderly or disabled member shall be entitled, with respect to expenses other than expenses paid on behalf of the household by a third party, to an excess medical expense deduction for the portion of the actual costs of allowable medical expenses, incurred by the elderly or disabled member, exclusive of special diets, that exceeds $35 per month.

(B) Method of claiming deduction

(i) In general

A State agency shall offer an eligible household under subparagraph (A) a method of claiming a deduction for recurring medical expenses that are initially verified under the excess medical expense deduction in lieu of submitting information on, or verification of, actual expenses on a monthly basis.

(ii) Method

The method described in clause (i) shall—

(I) be designed to minimize the burden for the eligible elderly or disabled household member choosing to deduct the recurrent medical expenses of the member pursuant to the method;

(II) rely on reasonable estimates of the expected medical expenses of the member for the certification period (including changes that can be reasonably anticipated based on available information about the medical condition of the member, public or private medical insurance coverage, and the current verified medical expenses incurred by the member); and

(III) not require further reporting or verification of a change in medical expenses if such a change has been anticipated for the certification period.

(7) Excess shelter expense deduction

(A) In general

A household shall be entitled, with respect to expenses other than expenses paid on behalf of the household by a third party, to an excess shelter expense deduction to the extent that the monthly amount expended by a household for shelter exceeds an amount equal to 50 percent of monthly household income after all other applicable deductions have been allowed.

(B) Maximum amount of deduction

In the case of a household that does not contain an elderly or disabled individual, in the 48 contiguous States and the District of Columbia,

Alaska, Hawaii, Guam, and the Virgin Islands of the United States, the excess shelter expense deduction shall not exceed—

(i) for the period beginning on August 22, 1996, and ending on December 31, 1996, $247, $429, $353, $300, and $182 per month, respectively;

(ii) for the period beginning on January 1, 1997, and ending on September 30, 1998, $250, $434, $357, $304, and $184 per month, respectively;

(iii) for fiscal year 1999, $275, $478, $393, $334, and $203 per month, respectively;

(iv) for fiscal year 2000, $280, $483, $398, $339, and $208 per month, respectively;

(v) for fiscal year 2001, $340, $543, $458, $399, and $268 per month, respectively; and

(vi) for fiscal year 2002 and each subsequent fiscal year, the applicable amount during the preceding fiscal year, as adjusted to reflect changes for the 12-month period ending the preceding November 30 in the Consumer Price Index for All Urban Consumers published by the Bureau of Labor Statistics of the Department of Labor.

(C) Standard utility allowance

(i) In general

In computing the excess shelter expense deduction, a State agency may use a standard utility allowance in accordance with regulations promulgated by the Secretary, except that a State agency may use an allowance that does not fluctuate within a year to reflect seasonal variations.

(ii) Restrictions on heating and cooling expenses

An allowance for a heating or cooling expense may not be used in the case of a household that—

(I) does not incur a heating or cooling expense, as the case may be;

(II) does incur a heating or cooling expense but is located in a public housing unit that has central utility meters and charges households, with regard to the expense, only for excess utility costs; or

(III) shares the expense with, and lives with, another individual not participating in the food stamp program, another household participating in the food stamp program, or both, unless the allowance is prorated between the household and the other individual, household, or both.

(iii) Mandatory allowance

(I) In general

A State agency may make the use of a standard utility allowance mandatory for all households with qualifying utility costs if—

(aa) the State agency has developed 1 or more standards that include the cost of heating and cooling and 1 or more standards that do not include the cost of heating and cooling; and

(bb) the Secretary finds that the standards will not result in an increased cost to the Secretary.

(II) Household election

A State agency that has not made the use of a standard utility allowance mandatory under subclause (I) shall allow a household to switch, at the end of a certification period, between the standard utility allowance and a deduction based on the actual utility costs of the household.

(iv) Availability of allowance to recipients of energy assistance

(I) In general

Subject to subclause (II), if a State agency elects to use a standard utility allowance that reflects heating or cooling costs, the standard utility allowance shall be made available to households receiving a payment, or on behalf of which a payment is made, under the Low-Income Home Energy Assistance Act of 1981 (42 U.S.C. 8621 et seq.) or other similar energy assistance program, if the household still incurs out-of-pocket heating or cooling expenses in excess of any assistance paid on behalf of the household to an energy provider.

(II) Separate allowance

A State agency may use a separate standard utility allowance for households on behalf of which a payment described in subclause (I) is made, but may not be required to do so.

(III) States not electing to use separate allowance

A State agency that does not elect to use a separate allowance but makes a single standard utility allowance available to households incurring heating or cooling expenses (other than a household described in subclause (I) or (II) of clause (ii)) may not be required to reduce the allowance due to the provision (directly or indirectly) of assistance under the Low-Income Home Energy Assistance Act of 1981 (42 U.S.C. 8621 et seq.).

(IV) Proration of assistance

For the purpose of the food stamp program, assistance provided under the Low-Income Home Energy Assistance Act of 1981 (42 U.S.C. 8621 et seq.) shall be considered to be prorated over the entire heating or cooling season for which the assistance was provided.

(f) Calculation of household income; prospective or retrospective accounting basis; consistency

(1)(A) Household income for those households that, by contract for other than an hourly or piecework basis or by self-employment, derive their annual income in a period of time shorter than one year shall be calculated by averaging such income over a twelve-month period. Notwithstanding the preceding sentence, household income resulting from the self-employment of a member in a farming operation, who derives income from such farming operation and who has irregular expenses to produce such income, may, at the option of the household, be calculated by averaging such income and expenses over a 12-month period. Notwithstanding the first sentence, if the averaged amount does not accurately reflect the household's actual monthly circumstances because the household has experienced a substantial increase or decrease in business earnings, the State agency shall calculate the self-employment income based on anticipated earnings.

(B) Household income for those households that receive nonexcluded income of the type described in subsection (d)(3) of this section shall be calculated by averaging such income over the period for which it is received.

(2)(A) Except as provided in subparagraphs (B), (C), and (D), households shall have their incomes calculated on a prospective basis, as provided in paragraph (3)(A), or, at the option of the State agency, on a retrospective basis, as provided in paragraph (3)(B).

(B) In the case of the first month, or at the option of the State, the first and second months, during a continuous period in which a household is certified, the State agency shall determine eligibility and the amount of benefits on the basis of the household's income and other relevant circumstances in such first or second month.

(c) Households specified in clauses (i), (ii), and (iii) of section 2015(c)(1)(A) of this title shall have their income calculated on a prospective basis, as provided in paragraph (3)(A).

(D) Except as provided in subparagraph (B), households required to submit monthly reports of their income and household circumstances under section 2015(c)(1) of this title shall have their income calculated on a retrospective basis, as provided in paragraph (3)(B).

(3)(A) Calculation of household income on a prospective basis is the calculation of income on the basis of the income reasonably anticipated to be received by the household during the period for which eligibility or benefits are being determined. Such calculation shall be made in accordance with regulations prescribed by the Secretary which shall provide for taking into account both the income reasonably anticipated to be received by the household during the period for which eligibility or benefits are being determined and the income received by the household during the preceding thirty days.

(B) Calculation of household income on a retrospective basis is the calculation of income for the period for which eligibility or benefits are being determined on the basis of income received in a previous period. Such calculation shall be made in accordance with regulations prescribed by the Secretary which may provide for the determination of eligibility on a prospective basis in some or all cases in which benefits are calculated under this paragraph. Such regulations shall provide for supplementing the initial allotments of newly applying households in those cases in which the determination of income under this paragraph causes serious hardship.

(4) In promulgating regulations under this subsection, the Secretary shall consult with the Secretary of Health and Human Services in order to assure that, to the extent feasible and consistent with the purposes of this chapter and the Social Security Act (42 U.S.C. 301 et seq.), the income of households receiving benefits under this chapter and title IV-A of the Social Security Act (42 U.S.C. 601 et seq.) is calculated on a comparable basis under this chapter and the Social Security Act. The Secretary is authorized, upon the request of a State agency, to waive any of the provisions of this subsection (except the provisions of paragraph (2)(A)) to the extent necessary to permit the State agency to calculate income for purposes of this chapter on the same basis that income is calculated under title IV-A of the Social Security Act in that State.

(g) Allowable financial resources which eligible household may own

(1) The Secretary shall prescribe the types and allowable amounts of financial resources (liquid and nonliquid assets) an eligible household may own, and shall, in so doing, assure that a household otherwise eligible to participate in the food stamp program will not be eligible to par-

ticipate if its resources exceed $2,000, or, in the case of a household which consists of or includes a member who is 60 years of age or older, if its resources exceed $3,000.

(2) Included assets.—

(A) In general.—

Subject to the other provisions of this paragraph, the Secretary shall, in prescribing inclusions in, and exclusions from, financial resources, follow the regulations in force as of June 1, 1982 (other than those relating to licensed vehicles and inaccessible resources).

(B) Additional included assets.—

The Secretary shall include in financial resources—

(I) any boat, snowmobile, or airplane used for recreational purposes;

(ii) any vacation home;

(iii) any mobile home used primarily for vacation purposes;

(iv) subject to subparagraphs (C) and (D), any licensed vehicle that is used for household transportation or to obtain or continue employment to the extent that the fair market value of the vehicle exceeds $4,650; and

(v) any savings or retirement acccunt (including an individual account), regardless of whether there is a penalty for early withdrawal.

(C) Excluded vehicles.—

A vehicle (and any other property, real or personal, to the extent the property is directly related to the maintenance or use of the vehicle) shall not be included in financial resources under this paragraph if the vehicle is—

(i) used to produce earned income;

(ii) necessary for the transportation of a physically disabled household member; or

(iii) depended on by a household to carry fuel for heating or water for home use and provides the primary source of fuel or water, respectively, for the household.

(D) Alternative vehicle allowance.—

If the vehicle allowance standards that a State agency uses to determine eligibility for assistance under the State program funded under part A of title IV of the Social Security Act (42 U.S.C. 601 et seq.) would result in a lower attribution of resources to certain households than under subparagraph (B)(iv), in lieu of applying subparagraph (B)(iv), the State agency may elect to apply the State vehicle allowance standards to all households that would incur a lower attribution of resources under the State vehicle allowance standards.

(3) The Secretary shall exclude from financial resources the value of a burial plot for each member of a household and nonliquid resources necessary to allow the household to carry out a plan for self-sufficiency approved by the State agency that constitutes adequate participation in an employment and training program under section 2015(d) of this title. The Secretary shall also exclude from financial resources any earned income tax credits received by any member of the household for a period of 12 months from receipt if such member was participating in the food stamp program at the time the credits were received and participated in such program continuously during the 12-month period.

(4) In the case of farm property (including land, equipment, and supplies) that is essential to the selfemployment of a household member in a farming operation, the Secretary shall exclude from financial resources the value of such property until the expiration of the 1-year period beginning on the date such member ceases to be self-employed in farming.

(5) The Secretary shall promulgate rules by which State agencies shall develop standards for identifying kinds of resources that, as a practical matter, the household is unlikely to be able to sell for any significant return because the household's interest is relatively slight or because the cost of selling the household's interest would be relatively great. Resources so identified shall be excluded as inaccessible resources. A resource shall be so identified if its sale or other disposition is unlikely to produce any significant amount of funds for the support of the household. The Secretary shall not require the State agency to require verification of the value of a resource to be excluded under this paragraph unless the State agency determines that the information provided by the household is questionable.

[Balance of Section Omitted]

SEC. 2015.—ELIGIBILITY DISQUALIFICATIONS

(a) Additional specific conditions rendering individuals ineligible

In addition to meeting the standards of eligibility prescribed in section 2014 of this title, households and individuals who are members of eligible households must also meet and comply with the specific requirements of this section to be eligible for participation in the food stamp program.

(b) Fraud and misrepresentation; disqualification penalties; ineligibility period; applicable procedures

(1) Any person who has been found by any State or Federal court or administrative agency to have intentionally

(A) made a false or misleading statement, or misrepresented, concealed or withheld facts, or

(B) committed any act that constitutes a violation of this chapter, the regulations issued thereunder, or any State statute, for the purpose of using, presenting, transferring, acquiring, receiving, or possessing coupons or authorization cards shall, immediately upon the rendering of such determination, become ineligible for further participation in the program—

(i) for a period of 1 year upon the first occasion of any such determination;

(ii) for a period of 2 years upon—

(I) the second occasion of any such determination; or

(II) the first occasion of a finding by a Federal, State, or local court of the trading of a controlled substance (as defined in section 802 of title 21) for coupons; and

(iii) permanently upon—

(I) the third occasion of any such determination;

(II) the second occasion of a finding by a Federal, State, or local court of the trading of a controlled substance (as defined in section 802 of title 21) for coupons;

(III) the first occasion of a finding by a Federal, State, or local court of the trading of firearms, ammunition, or explosives for coupons; or

---

(IV) a conviction of an offense under subsection (b) or (c) of section 2024 of this title involving an item covered by subsection (b) or (c) of section 2024 of this title having a value of $500 or more.

During the period of such ineligibility, no household shall receive increased benefits under this chapter as the result of a member of such household having been disqualified under this subsection.

[Balance of Section Omitted]

SEC. 2016.—ISSUANCE AND USE OF COUPONS

(a) Printing

Coupons shall be printed under such arrangements and in such denominations as may be determined by the Secretary to be necessary, and (except as provided in subsection (j) of this section) shall be issued only to households which have been duly certified as eligible to participate in the food stamp program.

(b) Approved food stores; receipt of cash in change for coupons used to purchase food

Coupons issued to eligible households shall be used by them only to purchase food in retail food stores which have been approved for participation in the food stamp program at prices prevailing in such stores: Provided, That nothing in this chapter shall be construed as authorizing the Secretary to specify the prices at which food may be sold by wholesale food concerns or retail food stores: Provided further, That eligible households using coupons to purchase food may receive cash in change therefor so long as the cash received does not equal or exceed the value of the lowest coupon denomination issued.

(c) Design of coupons

Coupons issued to eligible households shall be simple in design and shall include only such words or illustrations as are required to explain their purpose and define their denomination. The name of any public official shall not appear on such coupons.

[Sections "d" through "h" Omitted]

(i) Electronic benefit transfers

(1) In general.—

(A) Implementation.—

Not later than October 1, 2002, each State agency shall implement an electronic benefit transfer system under which household benefits determined under section 2017(a) or 2035 of this title are issued from and stored in a central databank, unless the Secretary provides a waiver for a State agency that faces unusual barriers to implementing an electronic benefit transfer system.

[Balance of Section Omitted]

SEC. 2017.—VALUE OF ALLOTMENT

(a) Calculation

The value of the allotment which State agencies shall be authorized to issue to any households certified as eligible to participate in the food stamp program shall be equal to the cost to such households of the thrifty food plan reduced by an amount equal to 30 per centum of the household's income, as determined in accordance with section 2014(d) and (e) of this title, rounded to the nearest lower whole dollar: Provided, That for households of one and two persons the minimum allotment shall be $10 per month.

[Balance of Section Omitted]

SEC. 2018.—APPROVAL OF RETAIL FOOD STORES AND WHOLESALE FOOD CONCERNS

(a) Applications; qualifications; certificate of approval; periodic reauthorization

(1) Regulations issued pursuant to this chapter shall provide for the submission of applications for approval by retail food stores and wholesale food concerns which desire to be authorized to accept and redeem coupons under the food stamp program and for the approval of those applicants whose participation will effectuate the purposes of the food stamp program. In determining the qualifications of applicants, there shall be considered among such other factors as may be appropriate, the following:

(A) the nature and extent of the food business conducted by the applicant;

(B) the volume of coupon business which may reasonably be expected to be conducted by the applicant food store or wholesale food concern; and

(C) the business integrity and reputation of the applicant. Approval of an applicant shall be evidenced by the issuance to such applicant of a nontransferable certificate of approval. No retail food store or wholesale food concern of a type determined by the Secretary, based on factors that include size, location, and type of items sold, shall be approved to be authorized or reauthorized for participation in the food stamp program unless an authorized employee of the Department of Agriculture, a designee of the Secretary, or, if practicable, an official of the State or local government designated by the Secretary has visited the store or concern for the purpose of determining whether the store or concern should be approved or reauthorized, as appropriate.

[Sections "b" through "d" Omitted]

(e) Reporting of abuses by public

Approved retail food stores shall display a sign providing information on how persons may report abuses they have observed in the operation of the food stamp program.

[Balance of Section Omitted]

SEC. 2019.—REDEMPTION OF COUPONS [OMITTED]

SEC. 2020.—ADMINISTRATION [OMITTED]

SEC. 2021.—CIVIL MONEY PENALTIES AND DISQUALIFICATION OF RETAIL FOOD STORES AND WHOLESALE FOOD CONCERNS

(a) Disqualification or civil penalty

Any approved retail food store or wholesale food concern may be disqualified for a specified period of time from further participation in the food stamp program, or subjected to a civil money penalty of up to $10,000 for each violation if the Secretary determines that its disqualification would cause hardship to food stamp households, on a finding, made as specified in the regulations, that such store or concern has violated any of the provisions of this chapter or the regulations issued pursuant to this chapter. Regulations issued pursuant to this chapter shall provide criteria for the finding of a violation and the suspension or disqualification of a retail food store or wholesale food concern on the basis of evidence that may include facts established through on-site investigations, inconsistent redemption data, or evidence obtained through a transaction report under an electronic benefit transfer system.

(b) Period of disqualification

Disqualification under subsection (a) of this section shall be—

(1) for a reasonable period of time, of no less than six months nor more than five years, upon the first occasion of disqualification;

(2) for a reasonable period of time, of no less than twelve months nor more than ten years, upon the second occasion of disqualification;

(3) permanent upon—

(A) the third occasion of disqualification;

(B) the first occasion or any subsequent occasion of a disqualification based on the purchase of coupons or trafficking in coupons or authorization cards by a retail food store or wholesale food concern, except that the Secretary shall have the discretion to impose a civil money penalty of up to $20,000 for each violation (except that the amount of civil money penalties imposed for violations occurring during a single investigation may not exceed $40,000) in lieu of disqualification under this subparagraph, for such purchase of coupons or trafficking in coupons or cards that constitutes a violation of the provisions of this chapter or the regulations issued pursuant to this chapter, if the Secretary determines that there is substantial evidence that such store or food concern had an effective policy and program in effect to prevent violations of the chapter and the regulations, including evidence that—

(i) the ownership of the store or food concern was not aware of, did not approve of, did not benefit from, and was not involved in the conduct of the violation; and

(ii)(I) the management of the store or food concern was not aware of, did not approve of, did not benefit from, and was not involved in the conduct of the violation; or

(II) the management was aware of, approved of, benefited from, or was involved in the conduct of no more than 1 previous violation by the store or food concern; or

(C) a finding of the sale of firearms, ammunition, explosives, or controlled substance (as defined in section 802 of title 21) for coupons, except that the Secretary shall have the discretion to impose a civil money penalty of up to $20,000 for each violation (except that the amount of civil money penalties imposed for violations occurring during a single investigation may not exceed $40,000) in lieu of disqualification under this subparagraph if the Secretary determines that there is substantial evidence (including evidence that neither the ownership nor management of the store or food concern was aware of, approved, benefited from, or was involved in the conduct or approval of the violation) that the store or food concern had an effective policy and program in effect to prevent violations of this chapter; and

(4) for a reasonable period of time to be determined by the Secretary, including permanent disqualification, on the knowing submission of an application for the approval or reauthorization to accept and redeem coupons that contains false information about a substantive matter that was a part of the application.

[Sections "c" through "e" Omitted]

(f) Fines for unauthorized third parties that accept food stamps

The Secretary may impose a fine against any person not approved by the Secretary to accept and redeem food coupons who violates any provision of this chapter or a regulation issued under this chapter, including violations concerning the acceptance of food coupons. The amount of any such fine shall be established by the Secretary and may be assessed and collected in accordance with regulations issued under this chapter separately or in combination with any fiscal claim established by the Secretary. The Attorney General of the United States may institute judicial action in any court of competent jurisdiction against the person to collect the fine.

(g) Disqualification of retailers who are disqualified under WIC program

(1) In general

The Secretary shall issue regulations providing criteria for the disqualification under this chapter of an approved retail food store or a wholesale food concern that is disqualified from accepting benefits under the special supplemental nutrition program for women, infants, and children established under section 1786 of title 42.

(2) Terms

A disqualification under paragraph (1)—

(A) shall be for the same length of time as the disqualification from the program referred to in paragraph (1);

(B) may begin at a later date than the disqualification from the program referred to in paragraph (1); and

(C) notwithstanding section 2023 of this title, shall not be subject to judicial or administrative review.

SEC. 2022.—DISPOSITION OF CLAIMS [OMITTED]

SEC. 2023.—ADMINISTRATIVE AND JUDICIAL REVIEW; RESTORATION OF RIGHTS [OMITTED]

SEC. 2024.—VIOLATIONS AND ENFORCEMENT [OMITTED]-:

SEC. 2025.—ADMINISTRATIVE COST-SHARING AND QUALITY CONTROL [OMITTED]

SEC. 2026.—RESEARCH, DEMONSTRATION, AND EVALUATIONS [OMITTED]

SEC. 2027.—APPROPRIATIONS AND ALLOTMENTS [OMITTED]

SEC. 2028.—PUERTO RICO BLOCK GRANT [OMITTED]

SEC. 2029.—WORKFARE

(a) Program plan; guidelines; compliance

(1) The Secretary shall permit any political subdivision, in any State, that applies and submits a plan to the Secretary in compliance with guidelines promulgated by the Secretary to operate a workfare program pursuant to which every member of a household participating in the food stamp program who is not exempt by virtue of the provisions of subsection (b) of this section shall accept an offer from such subdivision to perform work on its behalf, or may seek an offer to perform work, in return for compensation consisting of the allotment to which the household is entitled under section 2017(a) of this title, with each hour of such work entitling that household to a portion of its allotment

equal in value to 100 per centum of the higher of the applicable State minimum wage or the Federal minimum hourly rate under the Fair Labor Standards Act of 1938 (29 U.S.C. 201 et seq.).

(2)(A) The Secretary shall promulgate guidelines pursuant to paragraph (1) which, to the maximum extent practicable, enable a political subdivision to design and operate a workfare program under this section which is compatible and consistent with similar workfare programs operated by the subdivision.

(B) A political subdivision may comply with the requirements of this section by operating any workfare program which the Secretary determines meets the provisions and protections provided under this section.

(b) Exempt household members

A household member shall be exempt from workfare requirements imposed under this section if such member is—

(1) exempt from section 2015(d)(1) of this title as the result of clause (B), (C), (D), (E), or (F) of section 2015(d)(2) of this title;

(2) at the option of the operating agency, subject to and currently actively and satisfactorily participating at least 20 hours a week in a work activity required under title IV of the Social Security Act (42 U.S.C. 601 et seq.);

(3) mentally or physically unfit;

(4) under sixteen years of age;

(5) sixty years of age or older; or

(6) a parent or other caretaker of a child in a household in which another member is subject to the requirements of this section or is employed fulltime.

(c) Valuation or duration of work

No operating agency shall require any participating member to work in any workfare position to the extent that such work exceeds in value the allotment to which the household is otherwise entitled or that such work, when added to any other hours worked during such week by such member for compensation (in cash or in kind) in any other capacity, exceeds thirty hours a week.

(d) Nature, conditions, and costs of work

The operating agency shall—

(1) not provide any work that has the effect of replacing or preventing the employment of an individual not participating in the workfare program;

(2) provide the same benefits and working conditions that are provided at the job site to employees performing comparable work for comparable hours; and

(3) reimburse participants for actual costs of transportation and other actual costs all of which are reasonably necessary and directly related to participation in the program but not to exceed $25 in the aggregate per month.

(e) Job search period

The operating agency may allow a job search period, prior to making workfare assignments, of up to thirty days following a determination of eligibility.

(f) Disqualification

An individual or a household may become ineligible under section 2015(d)(1) of this title to participate in the food stamp program for failing to comply with this section.

[Balance of Section Omitted]

SEC. 2030.—WASHINGTON FAMILY INDEPENDENCE DEMONSTRATION PROJECT [OMITTED]

SEC. 2031.—FOOD STAMP PORTION OF MINNESOTA FAMILY INVESTMENT PLAN [OMITTED]

SEC. 2032.—AUTOMATED DATA PROCESSING AND INFORMATION RETRIEVAL SYSTEMS [OMITTED]

SEC. 2033.—TERRITORY OF AMERICAN SAMOA [OMITTED]

SEC. 2034.—ASSISTANCE FOR COMMUNITY FOOD PROJECTS

(a) "Community food projects" defined

In this section, the term "community food project" means a community-based project that requires a 1-time infusion of Federal assistance to become self-sustaining and that is designed to—

(1) meet the food needs of low-income people;

(2) increase the self-reliance of communities in providing for their own food needs; and

(3) promote comprehensive responses to local food, farm, and nutrition issues.

[Balance of Section Omitted]

SEC. 2035.—SIMPLIFIED FOOD STAMP PROGRAM [OMITTED]

SEC. 2036.—AVAILABILITY OF COMMODITIES FOR EMERGENCY FOOD ASSISTANCE PROGRAM [OMITTED] TO STATES FOR DISTRIBUTION IN ACCORDANCE WITH SECTION 7515 OF THIS TITLE.

APPENDIX 7:
DIRECTORY OF STATE FOOD STAMP INFORMATION NUMBERS

STATE	TELEPHONE NUMBER
Alabama	(334) 242-1700
Alaska	(907) 465-3360
Arizona	(800) 352-8401
Arkansas	(800) 482-8988
California	(800) 952-5253
Colorado	(303) 866-5087
Connecticut	(800) 842-1508
Delaware	(800) 464-4357
District of Columbia	(202) 724-5506
Florida	(800) 342-9274
Georgia	(800) 869-1150
Hawaii	(808) 586-5230
Idaho	(208) 334-5818
Illinois	(800) 252-8635
Indiana	(800) 622-4932
Iowa	(800) 972-2017
Kansas	(785) 296-3349
Kentucky	(800) 372-2973
Louisiana	(800) 256-1548
Maine	(800) 452-4643
Maryland	(800) 492-5515

STATE	TELEPHONE NUMBER
Massachusetts	(800) 645-8333
Michigan	(517) 373-0707
Minnesota	(800) 657-3698
Mississippi	(800) 948-3050
Missouri	(800) 392-2160
Montana	(800) 332-2272
Nebraska	(800) 430-3244
Nevada	(800) 992-0900
New Hampshire	(800) 852-3345
New Jersey	(800) 792-9773
New Mexico	(888) 473-3676
New York	(800) 342-3009
North Carolina	(800) 662-7030
North Dakota	(800) 755-2716
Ohio	(866) 244-0071
Oklahoma	(405) 521-3444
Oregon	(503) 945-6092
Pennsylvania	(800) 692-7462
Rhode Island	(800) 221-5689
South Carolina	(800) 768-5700
South Dakota	(877) 999-5612
Tennessee	(800) 342-1784
Texas	(800) 252-9330
Utah	(877) 817-1800
Vermont	(800) 287-0589
Virgin Islands	(340) 774-2399
Virginia	(800) 552-3431
Washington	(800) 865-7801
West Virginia	(800) 642-8589

STATE	TELEPHONE NUMBER
Wisconsin	(608) 266-2314
Wyoming	(800) 457-3657

APPENDIX 8:
FOOD STAMP INCOME ELIGIBILITY CHART

SIZE OF HOUSEHOLD	GROSS MONTHLY INCOME LIMITS	NET MONTHLY INCOME LIMITS
1	$931.00	$716.00
2	$1,258.00	$968.00
3	$1,585.00	$1,220.00
4	$1,913.00	$1,471.00
5	$2,240.00	$1,723.00
6	$2,567.00	$1,975.00
7	$2,894.00	$2,226.00
8	$3,221.00	$2,478.00
For each additional person add:	$328.00	$252.00

Note: Guidelines are subject to change therefore the reader is advised to check with the agency that administers the program for the most up-to-date information.

APPENDIX 9:
FOOD STAMP ALLOTMENT CHART

SIZE OF HOUSEHOLD	MAXIMUM MONTHLY ALLOTMENT
1	$135.00
2	$248.00
3	$356.00
4	$452.00
5	$537.00
6	$644.00
7	$712.00
8	$814.00
For Each Additional Person Add:	$102.00

Note: Guidelines are subject to change therefore the reader is advised to check with the agency that administers the program for the most up-to-date information.

APPENDIX 10:
STATE-FUNDED FOOD PROGRAMS FOR
LEGAL IMMIGRANTS

NOTE: The table below shows programs States have initiated to provide food assistance to legal immigrants who are ineligible for Federal Food Stamp benefits as a result of Welfare Reform.

STATE	STARTING DATE	TARGETED POPULATION
CALIFORNIA	9-1-97	Legal immigrants otherwise eligible.
CONNECTICUT	4-1-98	Legal immigrants otherwise eligible.
ILLINOIS	1-1-98	Parents of food-stamp eligible children; elderly (60-64); must have been in the U.S. as of 8/22/96.
MAINE	9-1-98	Legal immigrants otherwise eligible.
MARYLAND	10-1-97	Children under 18 arriving in the U.S. after 8/22/96.
MASSACHUSETTS	10-1-97	Legal immigrants otherwise eligible.
NEBRASKA	8-1-97	Legal immigrants otherwise eligible.
NEW JERSEY	3-10-99	Parents of food-stamp eligible children complying with work requirements; elderly (65 plus) arriving after 8/22/96.
NEW YORK	9-1-97	Elderly (60 - 67) living in the same county since 8/22/96.
RHODE ISLAND	10-1-98	Legal immigrants otherwise eligible.
WASHINGTON	11-1-99 STATE EBT	Legal immigrants otherwise eligible.
WISCONSIN	8-1-98	Legal immigrants otherwise eligible.

Note: Guidelines are subject to change therefore the reader is advised to check with the agency that administers the program for the most up-to-date information.

APPENDIX 11:

ADMINISTRATION FOR CHILDREN AND FAMILIES—STATE CHILD CARE AND DEVELOPMENT FUND CONTACTS

STATE	AGENCY	ADDRESS	TELEPHONE	FAX
ALABAMA	Department of Human Resources, Family Assistance Division	50 North Ripley Street, Montgomery, AL 36104	334-242-1773	334-242-0513
ALASKA	Department of Education and Early Development, Division of Early Development	333 West 4th Avenue, Suite 220, Anchorage, AK 99501-2341	907-269-4607	907-269-4635
ARKANSAS	Department of Human Services	101 East Capitol, Suite 106, Little Rock AR 72201	501-682-4891	501-682-4897
ARIZONA	Department of Economic Security, Child Care Administration	1789 W. Jefferson, 801A, Phoenix, AZ 85007	602-542-4248	602-542-4197
CALIFORNIA	Department of Education, Child Development Division	560 J Street, Suite 220, Sacramento, CA 95814-4785	916-324-8296	916-323-6853

STATE	AGENCY	ADDRESS	TELEPHONE	FAX
COLORADO	Department of Human Services, Division of Child Care	1575 Sherman Street, Denver, CO 80203-1714	303-866-5958	303-866-4453
CONNECTICUT	Department of Social Services, Family Services/Child Care Team	25 Sigourney Street, 10th Floor, Hartford, CT 06106-5033	860-424-5006	860-951-2996
DISTRICT OF COLUMBIA	Department of Human Services, Office of Early Childhood Development	717 14th Street NW, #750, Washington, DC 20005	202-727-1839	202-727-8166
DELAWARE	Herman Holloway Campus	1901 N. DuPont Highway, P.O. Box 906, New Castle, DE 19720	302-577-4880	302-577-4405
FLORIDA	Department of Children and Families, Family Safety and Preservation	1317 Winewood Blvd., Bldg. 7, Room 231, Tallahassee, FL 32399-0700	850-488-4900	850-488-9584
GEORGIA	Department of Human Resources, Division of Family and Children Services	Two Peachtree Street, NW, Suite 21-293, Atlanta, GA 30303	404-657-3438	404-657-3489
HAWAII	Department of Human Services	820 Mililani Street, Suite 606, Honolulu, HI 96813	808-586-7050	808-586-5229
IDAHO	Department of Health and Welfare, Division of Welfare	450 West State Street, 6th Floor, P.O. Box 83720, Boise, ID 83720-0036	208-334-5815	208-334-5817
ILLINOIS	Department of Human Services	330 Iles Park Place, Suite 270, Springfield, IL 62718	217-785-2559	217-524-6029

STATE	AGENCY	ADDRESS	TELEPHONE	FAX
INDIANA	Family & Social Services Administration, Bureau of Child Development	402 W. Washington Street, Indianapolis, IN 46204	317-232-1144	317-232-7948
IOWA	Department of Human Services, Division of ACFS	Hoover State Office Building, 5th Floor, Des Moines IA 50319-0114	515-281-4357	515-281-4597
KANSAS	Department of Social & Rehabilitation Services, Children and Family Policy Division	Docking State Office Bldg., 915 SW Harrison, Topeka, KS 66612	785-296-3349	785-296-0146
KENTUCKY	Cabinet for Families and Children, Department for Community Based Services	275 East Main Street, 3E-B6, Frankfort, KY 40621	502-564-2524	502-564-2467
LOUISIANA	Department of Social Services, Office of Family Support	P.O. Box 91193, Baton Rouge, LA 70821-9193	225-342-9106	225-342-9111
MAINE	Department of Human Services, Community Services Center	11 State House Station, Augusta, ME 04333-0011	207-287-5060	207-287-5031
MARYLAND	Department of Human Resources, Child Care Administration	311 W. Saratoga Street, 1st Floor, Baltimore, MD 21201	410-767-7128	410-333-8699
MASSACHUSETTS	Office of Child Care Services	One Ashburton Place, Room 1105, Boston, MA 02108	617-626-2000	617-626-2028

STATE	AGENCY	ADDRESS	TELEPHONE	FAX
MICHIGAN	Family Independence Agency	235 South Grand Ave., Suite 1302, P.O. Box 30037, Lansing, MI 48909-7537	517-373-0356	517-241-7843
MINNESOTA	Department of Children, Families & Learning	1500 Highway 36 West, Roseville, MN 55113-4266	651-582-8562	651-582-8496
MISSISSIPPI	Department of Human Services	750 North State Street, Jackson, MS 39202	601-359-4555	601-359-4422
MISSOURI	Department of Social Services	P.O. Box 88, Jefferson City, MO 65103	573-751-3221	573-751-0507
MONTANA	Department of Public Health and Human Services, Early Childhood Services Bureau	P.O. Box 202952, Helena, MT 59620-2952	406-444-1828	406-444-2547
NEBRASKA	Department of Health and Human Services, Resource Development and Support Unit	P.O. Box 95044, Lincoln, NE 68509-5044	402-471-9676	402-471-7763
NEVADA	Department of Human Resources, Welfare Division	2527 N. Carson Street, Carson City, NV 89706	775-687-1172	775-687-1079
NEW HAMPSHIRE	Department of Health and Human Services, Division for Children, Youth & Families	129 Pleasant Street, Concord, NH 03301-3857	603-271-8153	603-271-7982
NEW JERSEY	Department of Human Services, Division of Family Development	P.O. Box 716, Trenton, NJ 08625	609-588-2163	609-588-3051

STATE	AGENCY	ADDRESS	TELEPHONE	FAX
NEW MEXICO	Department of Children Youth and Families, Child Care Services Bureau	P.O. Drawer 5160, PERA Building, Room 111, Santa Fe, NM 87502-5160	505-827-9932	505-827-7361
NEW YORK	Department of Family Assistance, Office of Children and Family Services	40 North Pearl Street, Suite 11B, Albany, NY 12243	518-474-9324	518-474-9617
NORTH CAROLINA	Department of Health and Human Services, Division of Child Development	P.O. Box 29553, Raleigh, NC 27626-0553	919-662-4543	919-662-4568
NORTH DAKOTA	Department of Human Services, Office of Economic Assistance	State Capitol Judicial Wing, 600 East Boulevard Avenue, Bismarck, ND 58505-0250	701-328-2332	701-328-2359
OHIO	Department of Human Services	65 E. State Street, 5th Floor, Columbus, OH 43215	614-466-1043	614-728-6803
OKLAHOMA	Department of Human Services, Division of Child Care	Sequoyah Memorial Office Building, P.O. Box 25352, Oklahoma City, OK 73125-0352	405-521-3561	405-522-2564
OREGON	Department of Employment, Child Care Division	875 Union Street NE, Salem, OR 97311	503-947-1400	503-947-1428
PENNSYLVANIA	Department of Public Welfare, Office of Children, Youth & Families	Box 2675, Harrisburg, PA 17105-2675	717-787-8691	717-787-1529

STATE	AGENCY	ADDRESS	TELEPHONE	FAX
RHODE ISLAND	Department of Human Services	Louis Pasteur Bldg. #57, 600 New London Avenue, Cranston, RI 02920	401-462-3415	401-462-6878
SOUTH CAROLINA	Department of Health and Human Services, Bureau of Community Services	P.O. Box 8206, 1801 Main Street, 8th Floor, Columbia, SC 29202-8206	803-898-2570	803-898-4510
SOUTH DAKOTA	Department of Social Services, Child Care Services	700 Governors Drive, Pierre, SD 57501-2291	605-773-4766	605-773-6834
TENNESSEE	Department of Human Services	400 Deaderick Street, 14th Floor, Nashville, TN 37248-9600	615-313-4778	615-532-9956
TEXAS	Workforce Commission	101 East 15th Street, Suite 434T, Austin, TX 78778-0001	512-936-0474	512-936-3255
UTAH	Department of Workforce Services, Policy and Program Unit	140 East 300 South, Salt Lake City, UT 84111	801-526-9075	801-526-9211
VERMONT	Department of Social and Rehabilitation Services, Agency for Human Services	103 South Main Street, 2nd Floor, Waterbury, VT 05671-2401	802-241-3110	802-241-1220
VIRGINIA	Department of Social Services, Child Day Care	730 E. Broad St., Richmond, VA 23219-1849	804-692-1298	804-692-2209
WASHINGTON	Department of Social and Health Services, Division of Child Care and Early Learning	P.O. Box 45480, Olympia, WA 98504	360-413-3024	360-413-3482

STATE	AGENCY	ADDRESS	TELEPHONE	FAX
WEST VIRGINIA	Department of Health and Human Resources, Bureau for Children & Families	350 Capitol Street, Room 691, Charleston, WV 25301-3700	304-558-2993	304-558-8800
WISCONSIN	Department of Workforce Development	201 East Washington Avenue, Room 171, P.O. Box 7935, Madison WI 53707-7935	608-267-3708	608-261-6968
WYOMING	Department of Family Services	Hathaway Building, 2300 Capitol Avenue, ROOM 372, Cheyenne, WY 82002-0490	307-777-6848	307-777-7747

APPENDIX 12:
DIRECTORY OF HEAD START PROGRAM—STATE COLLABORATION OFFICES

STATE	AGENCY	ADDRESS	TELEPHONE	FAX
Alabama	Department of Children's Affairs	201 Monroe Street, Suite 1670, Montgomery, AL 36130-2755	334-223-0502	334-240-3054
Alaska	Head Start-State Collaboration Office, Department of Education and Early Development	333 West 4th Avenue, Suite 320, Anchorage, AK 99501	907-269-4518	none listed
Arizona	Head Start-State Collaboration Office, Governor's Division for Children	1700 West Washington, Suite 101-B, Phoenix, AZ 85007	602-542-3483	602-542-4644
Arkansas	Head Start-State Collaboration Office, Head Start Association	523 South Louisiana, Suite 301, Little Rock, AR 72201	501-371-0740	501-370-9109

STATE	AGENCY	ADDRESS	TELEPHONE	FAX
California	Head Start-State Collaboration Office, Department of Education	560 J Street, Suite 220, Sacramento, CA 95814	916-324-8296	916-323-6853
Colorado	Head Start-State Collaboration Office	136 State Capitol, Denver, CO 80203	303-866-4609	303-866-6368
Connecticut	Head Start-State Collaboration Office, Department of Social Services	25 Sigourney Street, Hartford, CT 06106	860-424-5066	860-424-4960
Delaware	Head Start-State Collaboration Office, Department of Education	Townsend Building, P.O. Box 1402, Dover, DE 19903	302-739-4667	302-739-2388
District of Columbia	Head Start-State Collaboration Office	717 Fourteenth Street NW, Suite 450, Washington, DC 20005	202-727-8113	202-727-8164
Florida	Head Start-State Collaboration Office, Collaboration for Young Children and Their Families	600 South Calhoun Street, Suite 146, Tallahassee, FL 32399-0240	850-414-7757	850-414-7760
Georgia	Head Start-State Collaboration Office, Office of School Readiness	10 Park Place South, Atlanta, GA 30303	404-656-5957	404-651-7184
Hawaii	Head Start-State Collaboration Office, Department of Human Services Benefit, Employment, and Support Services Division	820 Mililani Street, Suite 606, Honolulu, HI 96813	808-586-5240	808-586-5744

STATE	AGENCY	ADDRESS	TELEPHONE	FAX
Idaho	Head Start-State Collaboration Office, Head Start Association, Inc.	200 North 4th Street, Suite 20, Boise, ID 83702	208-345-1182	208-345-1163
Illinois	Head Start-State Collaboration Office, Department of Human Services	10 Collinsville Avenue, Suite 203, East St. Louis, IL 62201	618-583-2083	618-583-2091
Indiana	Head Start-State Collaboration Office	402 West Washington Street, Room W461, Indianapolis, IN 46204	317-233-6837	317-233-4693
Iowa	Head Start-State Collaboration Office, Department of Education	Grimes State Office Building, Des Moines, IA 50319-0146	515-242-6024	515-242-6019
Kansas	Head Start-State Collaboration Office, Department of Social and Rehabilitation Services	Docking State Office Building, 915 Southwest Harrison, Room 681 West, Topeka, KS 66612	785-368-6354	785-296-0146
Kentucky	Head Start-State Collaboration Office, Governor's Office of Early Childhood Development	275 East Main Street, Frankfort, KY 40621	502-564-8099	502-564-8330
Louisiana	Head Start-State Collaboration Office	412 4th Street, Room 105, Baton Rouge, LA 70802	225-219-4246	225-219-4248
Maine	Head Start-State Collaboration Office, Office of Child Care and Head Start	State House Station II, Augusta, ME 04333-0011	207-287-5060	207-287-5031

STATE	AGENCY	ADDRESS	TELEPHONE	FAX
Maryland	Head Start-State Collaboration Office, Governor's Office for Children, Youth and Families	301 West Preston Street, 15th Floor, Baltimore, MD 21201	410-767-4160	410-333-5248
Massachusetts	Head Start-State Collaboration Office, Executive Office of Health and Human Services	One Ashburton Place, Boston, MA 02108	617-727-7600	617-727-1396
Michigan	Head Start-State Collaboration Office, Family Independence Agency	235 South Grand Avenue, Suite 1302, P.O. Box 30037, Lansing, MI 48909	517-373-2492	517-241-9033
Minnesota	Head Start-State Collaboration Office, Department of Children, Families and Learning	1500 West Highway 36, Roseville, MN 55113	651-634-2203	651-582-8898
Mississippi	Head Start-State Collaboration Office	359 N. West Street, Jackson, MS 39205-0771	601-359-5798	601-359-1818
Missouri	Head Start-State Collaboration Office, Department of Human Development and Family Studies	1400 Rock Quarry Road, Columbia, MO 65211-3280	573-884-0579	573-884-0598
Montana	Head Start-State Collaboration Office	P.O. Box 202952, Helena, MT 59620-2952	406-444-0589	406-444-2547
Nebraska	Head Start-State Collaboration Office, Department of Education, Office of Children and Families	301 Centennial Mall South, P.O. Box 94987, Lincoln, NE 68509-4987	402-471-3501	402-471-0117

STATE	AGENCY	ADDRESS	TELEPHONE	FAX
Nevada	Head Start-State Collaboration Office, Department of Human Resources	3987 South McCarran Boulevard, Reno, NV 89502	775-688-2284	775-688-2558
New Hampshire	Head Start-State Collaboration Office, Department of Health and Human Services	129 Pleasant Street, Concord, NH 03301-6505	603-271-4454	603-271-7982
New Jersey	Head Start-State Collaboration Office, Office of Early Care and Education	P.O. Box 700, Trenton, NJ 08625-0700	609-984-5321	609-292-1903
New Mexico	Head Start-State Collaboration Office, Department of Children, Youth and Families	P.O. Drawer 5160, Sante Fe, NM 87502-5160	505-827-7499	505-827-7361
New York	Head Start-State Collaboration Office, Council on Children and Families	5 Empire State Plaza, Suite 2810, Albany, NY 12223-1553	518-474-6294	518-473-2570
North Carolina	Head Start-State Collaboration Office, Division of Child Development	319 Chapanoke Road, 2201 Mail Service Center 27699-2201, Raleigh, NC 27603	919-662-4543	919-662-4568
North Dakota	Head Start-State Collaboration Office, Department of Human Services	600 East Boulevard Avenue, Bismarck, ND 58505	701-328-1711	701-328-3538
Ohio	Head Start-State Collaboration Office, Office of Early Childhood Education	25 East Front Street, 3rd Floor, Columbus, OH 43215	614-466-0224	614-728-2538

STATE	AGENCY	ADDRESS	TELEPHONE	FAX
Oklahoma	Head Start-State Collaboration Office	2915 Classen, Suite 215, Oklahoma City, OK 73106	405-524-4124	405-524-4923
Oregon	Head Start-State Collaboration Office, Department of Education	255 Capitol Street NE, Salem, OR 97310-0203	503-378-3600	503-373-7968
Pennsylvania	Head Start-State Collaboration Office, Center for Schools and Communities	1300 Market Street, Suite 12, Lemoyne, PA 17043	717-763-1661	717-763-2083
Rhode Island	Head Start-State Collaboration Office, Department of Human Services	Louis Pasteur Building, 600 New London Avenue, Cranston, RI 02920	401-464-3071	401-462-6878
South Carolina	Head Start-State Collaboration Office, Department of Health and Human Services	1801 Main Street, 10th Floor, Columbia, SC 29201	803-898-2550	803-898-4513
South Dakota	Head Start-State Collaboration Office, Department of Education and Cultural Affairs	700 Governors Drive, Pierre, SD 57501-2291	605-773-4640	605-773-3782
Tennessee	Head Start-State Collaboration Office	Andrew Johnson Tower, 7th Floor, 710 James Robertson Parkway, Nashville, TN 37243-0376	615-741-4849	615-532-4989
Texas	Head Start-State Collaboration Office, Office of the Governor	7000 Fannin Street, Suite 2355, Houston, TX 77030	713-500-3835	none listed

STATE	AGENCY	ADDRESS	TELEPHONE	FAX
Utah	Head Start-State Collaboration Office, Child Adolescent and School Health Program	P.O. Box 142001, Salt Lake City, UT 84114-2001	801-538-9312	801-538-9409
Vermont	Head Start-State Collaboration Office, Agency of Human Services	103 South Main Street, Waterbury, VT 05671-0204	802-241-2705	802-241-2979
Virginia	Head Start-State Collaboration Office	700 Park Avenue, Norfolk, VA 23504	757-823-8322	757-823-2699
Washington	Governor's Head Start-State Collaboration Office, Division of Child Care and Early Learning	P.O. Box 45480, Olympia, WA 98504-5480	360-413-3330	360-413-3482
West Virginia	Head Start-State Collaboration Office, Governor's Cabinet on Children and Families	1900 Kanawha Boulevard East, Building 5, Room 218, Charleston, WV 25305	304-558-4638	304-558-0596
Wisconsin	Head Start-State Collaboration Office, Department of Workforce Development	201 E. Washington Avenue, Madison, WI 53707-7935	608-261-4596	608-267-3240
Wyoming	Head Start-State Collaboration Office	1465 North 4th Street, Suite 111, Laramie, WY 82072	307-766-2452	307-721-2084

APPENDIX 13:
U.S. DEPARTMENT OF HEALTH AND HUMAN SERVICES INFORMATION AND HOTLINE DIRECTORY

TOPIC	INTERNET ADDRESS	TELEPHONE
Adoption—National Adoption Information	Clearinghouse, www.acf.dhhs.gov/programs/cb,	888-251-0075
Adoption-Abductions	www.travel.state.gov/abduct.html	202-736-7000
Aging—Eldercare Info & Referrals	www.aoa.gov/elderpage.html	800-677-1116
Aging—Health Info & Research	www.nih.gov/nia	202-619-0724
AIDS/HIV	www.cdc.gov/hiv/dhap.htm	800-342-AIDS
Alcohol	www.niaaa.nih.gov	301-443-3860
Drug/Alcohol Abuse	www.nida.nih.gov	800-662-HELP
Allergies/Asthma	www.AAFA.orG	800-7-ASTHMA
Alzheimer's Disease	www.ninds.nih.gov/health	800-438-4380
Arthritis/Bone Diseases	www.nih.gov/niams	301-495-4484
Autism	www.ninds.nih.gov/health	301-496-5751
Birth Defects	www.nichd.nih.gov	301-496-5133
Blindness/Eye Information	www.nei.nih.gov	301-496-5248
Brain Tumors	www.nci.nih.gov	800-4-CANCER

TOPIC	INTERNET ADDRESS	TELEPHONE
Breast Cancer Information and Support	www.nci.nih.gov	800-4-CANCER
Breast Implants	www.fda.gov/cdrh/breastimplants/ index.html	301-8273990
Breastfeeding	www.mchb.hrsa.gov	301-443-3376
Cancer Information Service	cancernet.nci.nih.gov	800-4-CANCER
Cerebral Palsy	www.ninds.nih.gov	800-352-9424
Child Abuse and Neglect	www.acf.dhhs.gov/programs/cb	800-394-3366
Child Care Centers Information	www.acf.dhhs.gov/programs/ccb	800-598-KIDS
Child Health and Development	www.nichd.nih.gov	301-496-5133
Child Support Enforcement	www.acf.dhhs.gov/programs/CSE	202-401-9215
State Children's Health Insurance Program (SCHIP)	www.insurekidsnow.gov	877-KIDS-NOW
Childhood Immunization Information	www.cdc.gov/nip	800-232-2522
Children's Mental Health	www.nimh.nih.gov/publicat/ childmenu.cfm	800-789-2647
Children with Special Health Needs	www.acf.dhhs.gov/programs/add www.mchb.hrsa.gov/html/dscshn.html	202-401-9215
Chronic Diseases	www.cdc.gov/nccdphp/index.htm	800-311-3435
Civil Rights Offices	www.hhs.gov/ocr/ocrhmpg.html	800-368-1019
Clinical Practice Guidelines	www.clinicaltrials.gov	301-496-6308
Consumer Product Safety Hotline	www.cpsc.gov	800-638-2772
Cosmetics	http://vm.cfsan.fda.gov/~dms/cos-toc. html	800-270-8869

TOPIC	INTERNET ADDRESS	TELEPHONE
Deafness/Speech/ Communication Disorders	www.nidcd.nih.gov	800-241-1044
Dental/Tooth Decay	www.nidr.nih.gov	301-496-4261
Depression Helpline	www.nimh.nih.gov/publicat/ depressionmenu.cfm	800-421-4211
Developmental Disabilities	www.acf.dhhs.gov/programs/add	202-401-9215
Diabetes	www.niddk.nih.gov	301-654-3327
Digestive Diseases	www.niddk.nih.gov	301-654-3810
Disabled Children	www.cdc.gov/nceh/cddh/kids/kdhpage. htm	770-488-7150
Disease Prevention/Health Promotion	www.cdc.gov/nccdphp/index.htm	800-311-3435
Domestic Violence	www.cdc.gov/ncipc/dvp/vawprograms	800-799-SAFE
Drug/Alcohol— Information Only	www.health.org	800-729-6686 301-487-4889
Drug/Alcohol Treatment Referral Hotline	www.nida.nih.gov	800-662-HELP
Drug-Free Workplace	www.health.org/workplace	800-967-5752
Drugs-Adverse Reactions	www.fda.gov/medwatch	800-835-4709
Drugs—Prescription and OTC	www.fda.gov/cder	301-827-4573
Drug Use/Adolescents	www.monitoringthefuture.org	800-729-6686
Eldercare	www.aoa.gov/naic	800-677-1116
Energy Assistance	www.acf.dhhs.gov/programs	202-401-9215
Environmental Health	www.niehs.nih.gov	301-402-3378
Epilepsy	www.ninds.nih.gov	301-496-5751

TOPIC	INTERNET ADDRESS	TELEPHONE
Exercise	www.www.cdc.gov/nccdphp/dash/phactaaghtm	770-488-5820
Eye Information	www.nei.nih.gov	301-496-5248
Family Planning	www.hhs.gov/opa	301-654-6190
Food Safety	www.foodsafety.gov	1-888-SAFEFOOD
Foreign Medical Students	www.hrsa.gov	301-443-7194
Foster Care	www.acf.dhhs.gov/programs/cb	202-205-8618
Food and Drug Administration	www.fda.gov/foi/foia2.htm	202-690-7453
Genome Research	www.nhgri.nih.gov/NEWS/news.html	301-402-0911
Grief Helpline	www.nimh.nih.gov	301-443-4536
Handicapped/Developmental Disabilities	www.acf.dhhs.gov/programs/add	202-690-7888
Hazardous Substances	www.cdc.gov/niosh/homepage.html	800-35NIOSH
Headache	www.ninds.nih.gov	800-843-2256
Head Injury	www.ninds.nih.gov	800-352-9424
Head Start	www.acf.dhhs.gov/programs/hsb	202-205-8347
Health Care Technology	www.ahrq.gov	301-594-1364
Health Information	www.health.org	800-729-6686
Health Maintenance Orgs. (HMOs)	www.hcfa.gov/medicare/mgdcar.htm	800-MEDICARE
Health Professionals Education	www.hrsa.gov	800-ASK-HRSA
Herpes	www.niaid.nih.gov/default.htm	800-227-8922
High Blood Pressure/Cholesterol	www.nhlbi.nih.gov	301-251-1222
Hill Burton-funded Hospital Care	www.hrsa.gov	301-443-3376

TOPIC	INTERNET ADDRESS	TELEPHONE
HIV/AIDS	www.hcfa.gov/medicaid/hiv	202-690-6145
Homelessness	www.prainc.com/nrc/bibliographies/prevention.shtml	800-444-7415
Hospice	www.hcfa.gov/medicare/hosptc.htm	410-786-4154
Immunization Childhood	www.cdc.gov	800-232-2522
Indian Health Service	www.ihs.gov	301-443-3593
Infant Mortality/Healthy Start	www.mchb.hrsa.gov	800-311-BABY
Infectious Diseases Centers for Disease Control	www.cdc.gov/ncidod/index.htm	800-311-3435
International and Refugee Health	www.cdc.gov	301-443-1774
Juvenile Justice/U.S. Department of Justice	www.ojjdp.ncjrs.org	202-307-0703
Kidney/Urologic Diseases	www.niddk.nih.gov	301-654-4415
Lead Poisoning	www.niehs.nih.gov	800-424-LEAD
Learning Disabilities	www.ninds.nih.gov	301-496-5751
Leprosy (Hansen's Disease)	www.niaid.nih.gov	800-642-2477
Liver Diseases	www.niddk.nih.gov	301-654-3810
Lung Diseases	www.nhlbi.nih.gov	301-592-8523
Mammography	www.nci.nih.gov	800-332-8615
Marrow Donor Program	www.marrow.org	800-MARROW-2
Medicare	www.hcfa.gov/medicaid/medicaid.htm	800-MEDICARE
Medicaid/SCHIP	www.insurekidsnow.gov	877-KIDS-NOW
Medicaid/Medicare Fraud	www.hcfa.gov	800-HHS-TIPS

TOPIC	INTERNET ADDRESS	TELEPHONE
Medical Devices	www.fda.gov/cdrh/index.html	301-443-4190
Medical School Grants	www.hrsa.gov/bhpr	888-333-4774
Medicare (including Medigap)	www.hcfa.gov	800-MEDICARE
Medicine, National Library of	www.nlm.nih.gov	301-496-6308
Mental Health	www.samhsa.gov	800-789-2647
Mental Retardation	www.acf.dhhs.gov/programs/pcmr	202-401-9215
Migrant Worker Health Care	www.bphc.hrsa.gov	301-594-4303
Minority Health	www.omhrc.gov	301-443-5224
Missing Children/Runaways	www.missingkids.com	800-THE-LOST
National Health Service Corps	www.hrsa.gov	800-221-9393
National Practitioner Data Bank	www.hrsa.gov/bhpr	800-767-6732
Nutrition	www.fns.usda.gov/fncs	800-877-1600
Osteoporosis	www.osteo.org	800-624-BONE
Occupational Safety	www.osha.gov	800-356-4674
Organ and Other Transplantation	www.hrsa.gov/osp	888-90-SHARE
Outcomes Research	www.ahrq.gov	301-594-1364
Panic Disorder/Trauma Helpline	www.ninds.nih.gov	800-64-PANIC
Paralysis/Spinal Cord Injury	www.ninds.nih.gov	301-496-5751
Physical Fitness and Sports	www.cdc.gov/health/physact.htm	202-690-9000

TOPIC	INTERNET ADDRESS	TELEPHONE
Pregnancy/Prenatal Care	www.healthystart.net	301-443-0205
Pregnancy/Substance Abuse	www.health.org	800-622-4357
Product Problems	www.fda.gov/medwatch	800-332-1088
Radiological Health	www.fda.gov/cdrh	800-463-6332
Radon Safety Helpline	www.epa.gov/radonpro	800-SOS-RADON
Rape Crisis Hotline	www.bphc.hrsa.gov/omwh/ omwh_8.htm	800-656-HOPE
Recalls (foods, drugs, products)	www.cfsan.fda.gov	800-535-4555
Refugee Resettlement/ Immigration	www.acf.dhhs.gov/programs	202-401-9246
Reproductive Health	www.nichd.nih.gov	301-654-6190
Runaway Youth/Homelessness	www.nrscrisisline.org	800-621-4000
Rural Health Services	www.ruralhealth.hrsa.gov	301-443-083-7701
Ryan White Care Act	www.hrsa.gov/bhpr	301-443-6745
School Health Education	www.cdc.gov	800-311-3435
Seafood Hotline	vm.cfsan.fda.gov/list.html	1-888-SAFEFOOD
Sexually Transmitted Diseases Helpline	www.cdc.gov/nchstp/dstd/dstdp.html	800-227-8922
Sickle Cell Disease	www.SickleCelldisease.org	301-251-1222
SIDS (Sudden Infant Death Syndrome)	www.nichd.nih.gov/sids/sids.htm	800-638-7437
Smoking/Tobacco	www.health.org	404-639-3286
Spinal Cord Injury	www.ninds.nih.gov	301-496-5751

TOPIC	INTERNET ADDRESS	TELEPHONE
Statistics: Health Care and Vital	www.cdc.gov/nchs	301-458-4636
Stroke/Neurological Disorders	www.ninds.nih.gov	800-352-9424
Teen Pregnancy	www.teenpregnancy.org	202-478-8500*
Toxic Substances	www.niehs.nih.gov	919-541-3345
Travelers Health Information	www.cdc.gov/travel	877-394-8747
Treatment/Referral Assistance	www.ahrq.gov	800-358-9395
Uninsured Assistance	www.hcfa.gov/init/children.htm	301-443-3376
Urban Indian Health Programs	www.ihs.gov/nonmedicalprograms/urban/indian.asp	301-443-4680
Vaccine Adverse Events to Report	www.fda.gov/cber	800-822-7967
Vaccine Injury Compensation	www.bhpr.hrsa.gov/vicp/index.htm	800-338-2382
Veterinary Medicine	www.fda.gov/cvm/default.htm	301-594-1755
Weight Control/Obesity Information	www.niddk.nih.gov/health/nutrit/win.htm	877-946-4627
Welfare and AFDC Jobs Programs	www.acf.dhhs.gov/programs/cb	888-USA-JOB1
Women's Health Research	www.4woman.gov	800-994-9662
Youth Crisis Hotline	www.nrscrisisline.org	800-HIT-HOME

APPENDIX 14:

DIRECTORY OF ADMINISTRATION FOR CHILDREN AND FAMILIES (ACF)—REGIONAL OFFICES

REGION	AREA COVERED	TELEPHONE	FAX	ADDRESS	WEBSITE
REGION I—BOSTON	Connecticut, Maine, Massachusetts, New Hampshire, Rhode Island, Vermont	617-565-1020	617-565-2493	Administration for Children and Families, JFK Federal Building, Room 2000, 20th Floor, Boston, Massachusetts 02203-0001	http://www.acf.dhhs.gov/programs/nehub/index.htm

REGION	AREA COVERED	TELEPHONE	FAX	ADDRESS	WEBSITE
REGION II—NEW YORK	New York, Puerto Rico, Virgin Islands, New Jersey	212-264-2890	212-264-4881	Administration for Children and Families, 26 Federal Plaza, Room 4114, New York, New York 10278-0022	http://www.acf.dhhs.gov/programs/nehub/index.htm
REGION III—PHILADELPHIA	Delaware, Maryland, Pennsylvania, Virginia, West Virginia, District of Columbia	215-861-4000	215-861-4070	Administration for Children and Families, 150 S. Independence Mall West, Suite 864, Philadelphia, Pennsylvania 19106-3499	http://www.acf.dhhs.gov/programs/nehub/index.htm
REGION IV—ATLANTA	Alabama, Florida, Georgia, Kentucky, Mississippi, North Carolina, Tennessee, South Carolina	404-562-2900	404-562-2981	Administration for Children and Families, Atlanta Federal Center, 61 Forsyth St. SW, Suite 4M60, Atlanta, Georgia 30303-8909	http://www.acf.dhhs.gov/programs/sehub/index.htm

REGION	AREA COVERED	TELEPHONE	FAX	ADDRESS	WEBSITE
REGION V— CHICAGO	Illinois, Indiana, Michigan, Minnesota, Ohio, Wisconsin	312-353-4237	312-353-2204	Administration for Children and Families, 233 N. Michigan Avenue, Suite 400, Chicago, Illinois 60603	http://www.acf.dhhs.g ov/programs/mwhub/ index.html
REGION VI— DALLAS	Arkansas, Louisiana, New Mexico, Oklahoma, Texas	214-767-9648	214-767-3743	Administration for Children and Families, 1301 Young Street, Room 914, Dallas, Texas 75202	http://www.acf.dhhs. gov/programs/wchub/ index.htm
REGION VII— KANSAS CITY	Iowa, Kansas, Missouri, Nebraska	816-426-3981	816-426-2888	Administration for Children and Families, Federal Office Building, Room 276, 601 E. 12th Street, Kansas City, Missouri 64106-2898	http://www.acf.dhhs.g ov/programs/mwhub/ index.html

REGION	AREA COVERED	TELEPHONE	FAX	ADDRESS	WEBSITE
REGION VIII— DENVER	Colorado, Montana, North Dakota, South Dakota, Utah, Wyoming	303-844-3100	303-844-2624	Administration for Children and Families, Federal Office Building, 1961 Stout Street, Room 924, Denver, Colorado 80294-1185	http://www.acf.dhhs. gov/programs/wchub/ index.htm
REGION IX— SAN FRANCISCO	Arizona, California, Hawaii, Nevada, Guam, American Samoa, Trust Territory of Pacific Islands	415-437-8400	415-437-8444	Administration for Children and Families, 50 United Nations Plaza, Room 450, San Francisco, California 94102-4988	http://www.acf.dhhs. gov/programs/ pachub/index.html
REGION X— SEATTLE	Alaska, Idaho, Oregon, Washington	206-615-2547	206-615-2574	Administration for Children and Families, 2201 Sixth Avenue, Blanchard Plaza, Suite 600, Seattle, Washington 98121-1827	http://www.acf.dhhs. gov/programs/ pachub/index.html

APPENDIX 15:
DIRECTORY OF LOW INCOME HOME ENERGY ASSISTANCE PROGRAM (LIHEAP)—REGIONAL OFFICES

REGION	STATE	AGENCY	ADDRESS	TELEPHONE	FAX	WEBSITE	PUBLIC INQUIRIES
REGION 1							
	Connecticut	Department of Social Services	25 Sigourney Street, 10th Floor, Hartford, Connecticut 06106	(860) 424-5889	(860) 424-4952	www.dss.state.ct. us/svcs/energy.htm	(800) 842-1132
	Maine	State Housing Authority	353 Water Street, Augusta, Maine 04330	(207) 626-4600	(207) 624-5780	www.bundlemeup. org/grants.htm	(800) 452-4668

REGION	STATE	AGENCY	ADDRESS	TELEPHONE	FAX	WEBSITE	PUBLIC INQUIRIES
	Massachusetts	Bureau of Energy Programs/ DHCD	One Congress Street, 10th Floor, Boston, Massachusetts 02114	(617) 727-7004	(617) 727-4259	www.state.ma.us/ dhcd/components/ dns/HtOHA.htm	(800) 632-8175
	New Hampshire	Governor's Office of Energy and Community Services	57 Regional Drive, Concord, New Hampshire 03301-8519	(603) 271-8317	(603) 271-2615	www.state.nh.us/ governor/ energycomm/ assist.html	none listed
	Rhode Island	State Energy Office	One Capitol Hill, Providence, Rhode Island 02908-5850	(401) 222-6920	(401) 222-1260	none listed	(800) 253-4328
	Vermont	Office of Home Heating Fuel Assistance	103 South Main Street, Waterbury, Vermont 05676	(802) 241-2994	(802) 241-1394	www.dsw.state.vt. us/districts/fuel/ index.htm	(800)-479-6151
REGION 2	New Jersey	Home Energy Assistance Program, Division of Family Development	6 Quakerbridge Plaza, Trenton, New Jersey 08625	(609) 588-2478	(609) 588-3369	Www.state.nj.us /humanservices/df d/http://www.acf.h hs.gov/programs/ liheapl	(800) 510-3102

REGION	STATE	AGENCY	ADDRESS	TELEPHONE	FAX	WEBSITE	PUBLIC INQUIRIES
	New York	Division of Temporary Assistance, Department of Family Assistance	40 North Pearl Street, Albany, New York 12243-0001	(518) 473-0332	(518) 474-9347	www.otda.state. ny.us/otda/heap/ default.htm	(800) 342-3009
REGION 3							
	Delaware	Department of Health and Human Services	1901 N. Dupont Hwy, New Castle, Delaware 19720	(302) 255-9681	(302) 577-4973	none listed	(800) 464-HELP
	District of Columbia	Citizens Energy Resources Division	2000 14th St. N.W., Washington, D.C. 20001	(202) 673-6727	(202) 673-6725	www.dcenergy.org/ programs/fuel. htm#LIHEAP	(202) 673-6750
	Maryland	Department of Human Resources, Home Energy Programs	311 West Saratoga Street, Baltimore, Maryland 21202	(410) 767-7062	(410) 333-0079	www.dhr.state.md. us/meap	(800) 352-1446
	Pennsylvania	Division of Federal Programs, Department of Public Welfare	P.O. Box 2675, Harrisburg, Pennsylvania 17105	(717) 772-7906	(717) 772-6451	www.dpw.state.pa. us/oim/oimliheap. asp	(800) 692-7462

REGION	STATE	AGENCY	ADDRESS	TELEPHONE	FAX	WEBSITE	PUBLIC INQUIRIES
	Virginia	Energy Assistance Dept.	730 E. Broad Street, 7th Floor, Richmond, Virginia 23219-1849	(804) 692-1751	(804) 225-2196	www.dss.state.va. us/benefit/ energyasst.html	(800) 230-6977
	West Virginia	Department of Health and Human Resources, Office of Family Support	350 Capitol Street, Room B-18, Charleston, West Virginia 25301-3704	(304) 558-8290	(304) 558-2059	www.wvdhhr.org/ ofs/Utility.htm#LI EAP	304-558-8290
REGION 4							
	Alabama	Department of Economic and Community Affairs, Community Services Division	P. O. Box 5690, Montgomery, Alabama 36103-5690	(334) 242-5365	(334) 353-4311	none listed	none listed

REGION	STATE	AGENCY	ADDRESS	TELEPHONE	FAX	WEBSITE	PUBLIC INQUIRIES
	Florida	Division of Housing and Community Development, Department of Community Affairs	2555 Shumard Oak Boulevard, Tallahassee, Florida 32399-2100	(850) 922-1834	(850) 488-2488	www.dist. ct. App..state.fl.us/ fhcd/programs/ liheap	(850) 488-7541
	Georgia	Division of Family and Children Services	Two Peachtree Street, N.W., Suite 19-268, Atlanta, Georgia 30303-3180	(404) 463-2016	(404) 657-4480	www.state.ga.us/ departments/dhr/ energy.html	(800) 869-1150
	Kentucky	Energy Assistance Branch, Cabinet for Families and Children	275 East Main Street, 2nd Floor, Frankfort, Kentucky 40621	(502) 564-7536	(502) 564-0328	http://cfc.state.ky. us/help/liheap.asp	(800) 456-3452
	Mississippi	Department of Human Services, Division of Community Services	750 N. State Street, Jackson, Mississippi 39202-4772	(601) 359-4766	(601) 359-4370	www.mdhs.state. ms.us/cs_info.html	none listed

REGION	STATE	AGENCY	ADDRESS	TELEPHONE	FAX	WEBSITE	PUBLIC INQUIRIES
	North Carolina	Department of Health and Human Services, Division of Social Services	325 North Salisbury Street, Raleigh, North Carolina 27603-5905	(919) 733-7831	(919) 733-0645	www.dhhs.state. nc.us/dss	(800) 662-7030
	South Carolina	Division of Economic Opportunity	1205 Pendleton Street, Suite 342, Columbia, South Carolina 29201	(803) 734-9861	(803) 734-0356	none listed	none listed
	Tennessee	Department of Human Services	400 Deaderick Street, Nashville, Tennessee 37248	(615) 313-4764	(615) 532-9956	www.state.tn.us/ humanserv/ commsrv. htm#home	none listed
REGION 5							
	Illinois	Department of Commerce & Community Affairs	620 East Adams Street, Springfield, Illinois 62701	(217) 785–6135	none listed	www.commerce.sta te.il.us/com/ lowincome/ LIHEAP.htm	(800) 252-8643
	Indiana	Division of Children & Families	P.O. Box 6116, Indianapolis, Indiana 46206-6116	(317) 232-7015	(317) 232-7079	www.IN.gov/fssa/f amilies/housing/ eas.html	(800) 622-4973

REGION	STATE	AGENCY	ADDRESS	TELEPHONE	FAX	WEBSITE	PUBLIC INQUIRIES
	Michigan	Michigan Family Independence Agency	235 S. Grand Avenue, Lansing, Michigan 48909	(517) 241-7525	(517) 241-8053	www.michigan.gov/fia	(800) 292-5650
	Minnesota	Energy Assistance Programs, Energy Division	85 7th Place East, Suite 500, St. Paul, Minnesota 55101-2198	(651) 284-3275	(651) 284-3277	www.commerce.State.mn.us/pages/Energy/MainAssistance.htm	none listed
	Ohio	Department of Development	77 South High, 25th Floor, Columbus, Ohio 43216	(614) 644-6858	(614) 728-6832	www.odod.state.Oh.us/cdd/ocs/heap.htm	(800) 282-0880
	Wisconsin	Department of Administration, Energy Services	101 E. Wilson, 6th Floor, P.O. Box 7868, Madison, Wisconsin 53707-7868	(608) 2667601	(608) 264-6688	www.doa.state.wi.us/depb/boe/index.asp	(608) 267-3680
REGION 6	Arkansas	Department of Human Services, Home Energy Assistance Program	P.O. Box 1437, Little Rock, Arkansas 72203-1437	(501) 682-8726	(501) 682-6736	www.state.ar.us/dhs/dco/ocs/index.htm#haap	(800) 432-0043

REGION	STATE	AGENCY	ADDRESS	TELEPHONE	FAX	WEBSITE	PUBLIC INQUIRIES
	Louisiana	Louisiana Housing Finance Agency, Energy Assistance Department	2415 Quail Drive, Baton Rouge, Louisiana 70808	(225) 763-8700	(225) 763-8710	www.lhfa.state.la.us	(225) 342-2288
	New Mexico	Human Services Department, Income Support Division	5301 Central NE, Suite 1520, Albuquerque, New Mexico 87108	(505) 841-6535	(505) 841-6522	www.state.nm.us/hsd/isd.html	(800) 283-4465
	Oklahoma	Department of Human Services, Division of Family Support Services	P.O. Box 25352, Oklahoma City, Oklahoma 73125	(405) 521-4488	(405) 521-4158	none listed	none listed
	Texas	Department of Housing and Community Affairs, Energy Assistance Section	P.O. Box 13941, Austin, Texas 78711-3941	(512) 475-3864	(512) 475-3935	www.tdhca.state.tx.us/ea.htm	(877) 399-8939

REGION	STATE	AGENCY	ADDRESS	TELEPHONE	FAX	WEBSITE	PUBLIC INQUIRIES
REGION 7							
	Iowa	Department of Human Rights, Division of Community Action Agencies	Des Moines, Iowa 50319	(515) 281-0859	(515) 242-6119	www.state.ia.us/government/dhr/caa	(515) 281-4204
	Kansas	Social & Rehabilitation Services	915 SW Harrison, Topeka, Kansas 66612-1505	(785) 368-8115	(785) 368-8114	www.srskansas.org/ees/lieap.htm	(800) 432-0043
	Missouri	Department of Social Services, Division of Family Services	P.O. Box 88, Jefferson City, Missouri 65103	(573) 751-0472	(573) 526-5592	www.dss.state.mo.us/dfs/http://www.acf.hhs.gov/programs/liheap	(800) 392-1261
	Nebraska	Department of Health and Human Services, Program Assistance Unit	301 Centennial Mall South, 4th Floor, P.O. Box 95026, Lincoln, Nebraska 68509	(402) 471-9262	(402) 471-9597	www.hhs.state.ne.us/fia/energy.htm	(800) 430-3244
REGION 8							

REGION	STATE	AGENCY	ADDRESS	TELEPHONE	FAX	WEBSITE	PUBLIC INQUIRIES
	Colorado	Department of Human Services, Office of Self-Sufficiency	1575 Sherman Street, 3rd Floor, Denver, Colorado 80203	(303) 866-5968	(303) 866-5488	www.cdhs.state.co.us/oss/FAP/LEAP/LEAPhtm	(800) 782-0721
	Montana	Department of Public Health and Human Services, Intergovernmental Human Services Bureau	1400 Carter Drive, Helena, Montana 59620	(406) 447-4260	(406) 447-4287	none listed	(800) 332-2272
	North Dakota	Department of Human Services	600 E. Boulevard, Dept. 325, Bismarck, North Dakota 58505-0250	(701) 328-4882	(701) 328-1060	http://lnotes.state.nd.us/dhs/dhsweb.nsf	(701) 328-2065
	South Dakota	Department of Social Services, Office of Energy Assistance	206 W. Missouri Avenue, Pierre, South Dakota 57501-4517	(605) 773-4131	(605) 773-6657	www.state.sd.us/social/ENERGY	(800) 233-8503

REGION	STATE	AGENCY	ADDRESS	TELEPHONE	FAX	WEBSITE	PUBLIC INQUIRIES
	Utah	Department of Community and Economic Development	324 South State, Suite 500, Salt Lake City, Utah 84111	(801) 538-8644	(801) 538-8888	www.dced.state.ut. us/community/ heat.html	(877) 488-3233
	Wyoming	Department of Family Services	2300 Capitol Avenue, Room 388, Cheyenne, Wyoming 82002-0490	(307) 777-6346	(307) 777-7747	http://dfsweb.state. wy.us/fieldop/ briefing5a.htm	(800) 246-4221
REGION 9							
	Arizona	Arizona Department of Economic Security, Community Services Administration	1789 W. Jefferson, P.O. Box 6123, Phoenix, Arizona 85007	(602) 542-6600	(602) 364-1756	www.de.state.az. Us/links/csa_web/ index.asp	(800) 582-5706
	California	Department of Community Services and Development	700 North 10th Street, Room 258, Sacramento, California 95814	(916) 341-4327	(916) 327-3153	www.csd.ca.gov/ http://www.acf.hhs. gov/programs/ liheap	(800) 433-4327

REGION	STATE	AGENCY	ADDRESS	TELEPHONE	FAX	WEBSITE	PUBLIC INQUIRIES
	Hawaii	Department of Human Services, Benefit, Employment and Support Division	820 Mililani Street, Suite 606, Honolulu, Hawaii 96813	(808) 586-5734	(808) 586-5744	none listed	(808) 586-5740
	Nevada	Department of Human Resource, State Welfare Division	559 S. Saliman Rd., Suite 101, Carson City, Nevada 89701-5040	(775) 687-6919	(775) 687-1272	http://welfare.state. nv.us/benefit/ lihea.htm	(800) 992-0900
REGION 10							
	Alaska	Department of Health and Social Services, Division of Public Assistance	400 W. Willoughby Ave., Room 301, Juneau, Alaska 99801-1700	(907) 465-3066	(907) 465-3319	www.hss.state.ak. us/dpa/programs/ hap.html	(800) 470-3058

REGION	STATE	AGENCY	ADDRESS	TELEPHONE	FAX	WEBSITE	PUBLIC INQUIRIES
	Idaho	Department of Health and Welfare, Bureau of Benefit Program Operations	P.O. Box 83720, Boise, Idaho 83720-0036	(208) 334-5753	(208) 332-7343	none listed	(208) 334-5730
	Oregon	Department of Housing and Community Services	1600 State Street, Salem, Oregon 97310	(503) 986-2094	(503) 986-2006	www.hcs.state.or. us/community_ resources/energy_ wx/index.html	(800) 453-5511
	Washington	Department of Community Trade and Economic Development	906 Columbia Street S.W., P.O. Box 48300, Olympia, Washington 98504-8300	(360) 725-2854	(360) 586-0489	www.liheapwa.org	(360) 725-2854

GLOSSARY

Adoption Opportunities Program—A program designed to eliminate barriers to adoption and help find permanent homes for children, particularly those with special needs, who would benefit by adoption.

Alimony—All periodic payments people receive from ex-spouses, excluding one-time property settlements.

Allotment—As it refers to food stamps, means the total value of coupons a household is authorized to receive during each month.

Allowable Medical Expenses—As it refers to food stamp eligibility, means expenditures for (1) medical and dental care, (2) hospitalization or nursing care, (3) prescription drugs prescribed by a licensed practitioner authorized under State law and over-the-counter medication when approved by a licensed practitioner or other qualified health professional, (4) health and hospitalization insurance policies, (5) medicare premiums related to coverage under title XVIII of the Social Security Act, (6) dentures, hearing aids, and prosthetics, (7) eye glasses prescribed by a physician skilled in eye disease or by an optometrist, (8) reasonable costs of transportation necessary to secure medical treatment or services, and (9) maintaining an attendant, homemaker, home health aide, housekeeper, or child care services due to age, infirmity, or illness.

Assets—The entirety of a person's property, either real or personal.

Authorization Card—The document issued by the State agency to an eligible household which shows the food stamp allotment the household is entitled to be issued.

Birth Cohort—A birth cohort is a group of people who were born in a specified calendar period.

Capacity—Capacity is the legal qualification concerning the ability of one to understand the nature and effects of one's acts.

Certification period—The period for which households shall be eligible to receive food stamp authorization cards.

Child Abuse—Any form of cruelty to a child's physical, moral or mental well-being.

Child Custody—The care, control and maintenance of a child which may be awarded by a court to one of the parents of the child.

Child Protective Agency—A state agency responsible for the investigation of child abuse and neglect reports.

Children—All persons under 18 years, excluding people who maintain households, families, or subfamilies.

Children Ever Born—Term used to refer to the number of children born to a women before her present marriage, children no longer living, and children away from home as well as children who are still living in the home.

Child support—All periodic payments a parent receives from an absent parent for the support of children, even if these payments are made through a state or local government office.

Child Welfare—A generic term which embraces the totality of measures necessary for a child's well being; physical, moral and mental.

Child Welfare Services—Services directed toward the goal of keeping families together. They include preventive intervention so that, if possible, children will not have to be removed from their homes. If this is not possible, placements and permanent homes through foster care or adoption can be made. Reunification services are available to encourage the return home, when appropriate, of children who have been removed from their families

Citizenship status—The five categories of citizenship status include: 1) Born in the United States; 2) Born in Puerto Rico or another outlying area of the U.S.; 3) Born abroad of U.S. citizen parents; 4) Naturalized citizens; 5) Non-citizens.

Community Spouse—Community-dwelling spouse of an institutionalized person.

Community Spouse Protected Resource Amount (CSRA)—Amount to which the spousal share is compared for protection against spousal impoverishment.

Coupon—Refers to any coupon, stamp, type of certificate, authorization card, cash, check or access device, including an electronic benefit transfer card or personal identification number, issued in connection with the food stamp program.

Disability—Under the Social Security or Supplemental Security Income government programs, refers to the inability to do any substantial gainful activity because of a medically provable physical or mental impairment that is expected to result in death, or that has lasted, or is expected to last, at least 12 continuous months.

Disability Benefits—Payments people receive as a result of a health problem or disability.

Dividends—Income people receive from stock holdings and mutual fund shares.

Drug addiction or Alcoholic Treatment and Rehabilitation Program —Any program conducted by a private nonprofit organization or institution, or a publicly operated community mental health center, to provide treatment that can lead to the rehabilitation of drug addicts or alcoholics.

Dual Eligibles—Individuals who are entitled to Medicare Part A and/or Part B and are also eligible for some form of Medicaid benefit.

Earned Income—Income which is gained through one's labor and services, as opposed to investment income.

Educational Assistance—Pell Grants; other government educational assistance; any scholarships or grants; or financial assistance students receive from employers, friends, or relatives not residing in the student's household.

Educational Attainment—The highest grade of school completed, or the highest degree received.

Electronic Benefit Transfer Card—A card that provides benefits under the Food Stamp Program through an electronic benefit transfer service.

Electronic Benefit Transfer Contract—A contract that provides for the issuance, use, or redemption of coupons in the form of electronic benefit transfer cards.

Emancipation—The surrender of care, custody and earnings of a child, as well as renunciation of parental duties.

Family—A family is a group of two people or more related by birth, marriage, or adoption and residing together.

Financial Assistance from Outside of the Household—Periodic payments people receive from non-household members, excluding gifts or sporadic assistance.

Food—Any food or food product for home consumption except alcoholic beverages, tobacco, and hot foods or hot food products ready for immediate consumption.

Food Stamp Program—The program operated pursuant to the provisions of The Federal Food Stamp Act, Title 7, Chapter 51, to permit low-income households to obtain a more nutritious diet through normal channels of trade by increasing food purchasing power for all eligible households who apply for participation.

Government Transfers—Payments people receive from: (1) unemployment compensation, (2) state workers' compensation, (3) social security, (4) Supplemental Security Income (SSI), (5) public assistance, (6) veterans' benefits, (7) government survivor benefits, (8) government disability benefits, (9) government pensions, and (10) government educational assistance.

Group quarters—Noninstitutional living arrangements for groups not living in conventional housing units.

Guardian—A person who is entrusted with the management of the property and/or person of another who is incapable, due to age or incapacity, to administer their own affairs.

Head Start—Program designed to provide preschool education to young children. Every child receives a variety of learning experiences to foster intellectual, social, and emotional growth. Head Start emphasizes the importance of the early identification of health«problems. Every child is involved in a comprehensive health program, which includes immunizations, medical, dental, and mental health, and nutritional services.

Homeless Individual—An individual who lacks a fixed and regular nighttime residence; or an individual who has a primary nighttime residence that is: (A) a supervised publicly or privately operated shelter designed to provide temporary living accommodations; (B) an institution that provides a temporary residence for individuals intended to be institutionalized; (C) a temporary accommodation for not more than 90 days in the residence of another individual; or (D) a public or private place not designed for, or ordinarily used as, a regular sleeping accommodation for human beings.

Household—All the people who occupy a housing unit, including the related family members and all the unrelated people.

Income—The amount of money income received in the preceding calendar year from each of the following sources (1) Earnings; (2) Unemployment compensation; (3) Workers' compensation; (4) Social security; (5)

Supplemental security income; (6) Public assistance; (7) Veterans' payments; (8) Survivor benefits; (9) Disability benefits; (10) Pension or retirement income; (11) Interest; (12) Dividends; (13) Rents, royalties, and estates and trusts; (14) Educational assistance; (15) Alimony; (16) Child support; (18) Financial assistance from outside of the household; and (19) Other income.

Income Standard—The maximum amount of income a person can have and still be eligible for certain public assistance programs.

Income-to-Poverty Ratios—Income-to-poverty ratios represent the ratio of family or unrelated individual income to their appropriate poverty threshold.

Indigent—A person who is financially destitute.

In Loco Parentis—Latin for "in the place of a parent." Refers to an individual who assumes parental obligations and status without a formal, legal adoption.

Interest Income—Payments people receive from bonds, treasury notes, IRAs, certificates of deposit, interest-bearing savings and checking accounts, and all other investments that pay interest.

Interoperability—A system that enables a coupon issued in the form of an electronic benefit transfer card to be redeemed in any State.

Interstate Transaction—A transaction that is initiated in one State by the use of an electronic benefit transfer card that is issued in another State.

Marital Status—Marital status classifications of (1) never married; (2) married; (3) widowed; and (4) divorced.

Mean Income—Mean income is the amount obtained by dividing the total aggregate income of a group by the number of units in that group.

Median Income—Median income is the amount which divides the income distribution into two equal groups, half having incomes above the median, half having incomes below the median.

Minor—A person who has not yet reached the age of legal competence, which is designated as 18 in most states.

Out of Wedlock Birth—Out-of-wedlock births are defined as births to women who were currently divorced, widowed, or never married at the time of birth.

Parens Patriae—Latin for "parent of his country." Refers to the role of the state as guardian of legally disabled individuals.

Paternity—The relationship of fatherhood.

Per Capita Income—Per capita income is the average income computed for every man, woman, and child in a particular group.

Personal Needs Allowance—Limited amount of income a nursing facility resident is allowed to keep for monthly expenses.

Portability—A system that enables a coupon issued in the form of an electronic benefit transfer card to be used in any State by a household to purchase food at an approved retail food store or wholesale food concern.

Public assistance (Welfare)—Cash public assistance payments to low-income people receive, such as aid to families with dependent children (AFDC), temporary assistance to needy families (TANF), general assistance, and emergency assistance.

Reconstituted Family—A family in which the original parent has divorced and remarried.

Rents, royalties, and Estates and Trusts—Net income people receive from the rental of a house, store, or other property, receipts from boarders or lodgers, net royalty income, and periodic payments from estate or trust funds.

Resource Standard—The maximum amount of resources a person can have and still be eligible for certain public assistance programs.

Selective Emancipation—The doctrine under which a child is deemed emancipated for only a part of the period of minority, or from only a part of the parent's rights, or for some purposes, and not for others.

Single Parent Family—A family in which one parent remains the primary caretaker of the children, and the children maintain little or no contact with the other parent.

Size of Household—The term "size of household" includes all the people occupying a housing unit.

Social Security—Includes social security pensions and survivors' benefits and permanent disability insurance payments made by the Social Security Administration prior to deductions for medical insurance.

Special Income Rule—State option to provide Medicaid to persons in institutions who have too much income to qualify for SSI benefits, but not enough income to cover their expensive long-term care.

Spend Down Provision—Process in which individuals become Medicaid-eligible by incurring high medical bills which reduce the individual's income below the state-determined income eligibility limit.

Spousal Impoverishment Protections—Process designed to ensure that when one spouse is institutionalized for at least 30 days, the other spouse does not lose all income and resources, thereby becoming impoverished and needing public assistance.

Spousal Share—Amount determined when the couple's resources, excluding their home, household goods, one automobile, and burial funds, are combined and then divided in half to determine the spousal impoverishment protection.

Staple Foods—Refers to foods in the categories of meat, poultry, fish, bread, cereals, vegetables, fruits, dairy products, not including accessory food items, such as coffee, tea, cocoa, carbonated and uncarbonated drinks, candy, condiments, and spices.

State Agency—The agency of State government, including the local offices thereof, which has the responsibility for the administration of the federally aided public assistance programs within such State, including any counterpart local agencies administering such programs.

State Supplementary Payments—Amount by which a state may opt to supplement the basic Supplemental Security Income cash assistance payments.

Supplemental Security Income (SSI)—Federal, state, and local welfare agency payments to low-income people who are 65 years old and over or people of any age who are blind or disabled.

Survivor Benefits—Payments people receive from survivors' or widows' pensions, estates, trusts, annuities, or any other types of survivor benefits.

Unemployment Compensation—Payments people receive from government unemployment agencies or private companies during periods of unemployment and any strike benefits the person receives from union funds.

Unmarried Couple—An unmarried couple is composed of two unrelated adults of the opposite sex who share a housing unit.

Unrelated Individuals—Unrelated individuals are people of any age who are not members of families or subfamilies.

Veterans' Payments—Payments disabled members of the armed forces or survivors of deceased veterans receive periodically from the Department of Veterans Affairs for education and on-the-job training, and means-tested assistance to veterans.

Ward—A person over whom a guardian is appointed to manage his or her affairs.

Workers' Compensation—Payments people receive periodically from public or private insurance companies for injuries received at work.

Work Experience—A person with work experience is one who, during the preceding calendar year, did any work for pay or profit or worked without pay on a family-operated farm or business at any time during the year, on a part-time or full-time basis.

BIBLIOGRAPHY AND ADDITIONAL READING

The Administration on Aging (Date Visited: August 2002) <http://www.aoa.gov/>.

Black's Law Dictionary, Fifth Edition. St. Paul, MN: West Publishing Company, 1979.

The Head Start Program (Date Visited: August 2002) <http://www2.acf.dhhs.gov/programs/hsb/index.htm/>.

The Social Security Administration (Date Visited: August 2002) <http://www.socialsecurity.gov/>.

The State Children's Health Insurance Program (SCHIP) (Date Visited: August 2002) <http://www.insurekidsnow.gov/>.

The United States Census Bureau (Date Visited: August 2002) <http://www.census.gov/>.

The United States Department of Agriculture, Food and Nutrition Services, Food Stamp Program (Date Visited: August 2002) <http://www.fns.usda.gov/fsp/>.

The United States Department of Health and Human Services, Administration for Children and Families (Date Visited: August 2002) <http://www.acf.dhhs.gov/>.

The United States Department of Health and Human Services, Office of Child Support Enforcement (Date Visited: August 2002) <http://www.acf.dhhs.gov/cse/programs.>.

The United States Department of Labor, Welfare to Work Program (Date Visited: August 2002) <http://wtw.doleta.gov/>.